By the North Sea

By the North Sea

An Anthology
of Suffolk Poetry

edited by
Aidan Semmens

Shearsman Books

First published in the United Kingdom in 2013 by
Shearsman Books
50 Westons Hill Drive
Emersons Green
BRISTOL
BS16 7DF

Shearsman Books Ltd Registered Office
30–31 St. James Place, Mangotsfield, Bristol BS16 9JB
(this address not for correspondence)

www.shearsman.com

ISBN 978-1-84861-285-3
First Edition

Introduction copyright © Ronald Blythe, 2013.
Introduction and selection copyright © Aidan Semmens, 2013.

Copyright in the poems gathered here in Part 2 remains
with the authors concerned, or their Estates. We are grateful to the original
publishers for permission to reprint the poems here. Full details of the sources for
the poems may be found in the Acknowledgements on pages 126-127.

Contents

| Ronald Blythe | Foreword | 7 |
| Aidan Semmens | Introduction | 8 |

The Poets
Algernon Charles Swinburne	15
Henry Howard, Earl of Surrey	17
Ann Candler	20
Anna Laetitia Barbauld	25
George Crabbe	29
Robert Bloomfield	40
Bernard Barton	45
Andy Brown	49
Angela Leighton	52
Tamar Yoseloff	54
Ronald Blythe	56
Victor Tapner	58
Pauline Stainer	61
John Matthias	67
Wendy Mulford	78
Claire Crowther	82
R.F. Langley	83
Andrew Brewerton	87
Rodney Pybus	88
Charlotte Geater	92
Zoë Skoulding	94
Deryn Rees-Jones	96
Aidan Semmens	97
Michael Laskey	102
Herbert Lomas	104
Anne Beresford	107
Will Stone	110
Richard Caddel	112
Michael Hamburger	113
Biographical Notes	118
Acknowledgements	126

Foreword

Ronald Blythe

The anthologist must represent the expected and the surprising, the old and the new, particularly when a collection aims to reveal a people and a place. As does *By the North Sea*. And of course neither artist nor writer need be indigenous to Suffolk to show its seemingly contradictory element of being wide open yet mysterious. Thus we have its master voice, George Crabbe, and a host of incomers whose work sweeps away the clichés which dull the county, and makes us look at it afresh through their eyes.

One of the skills demanded of the good anthologist is how to include a classic long poem, all of it or some of it? And here Aidan Semmens shows both his own delight in it and his editorial skill and judgment. Thus we have all of *Peter Grimes*, that remorselessly terrible tale. It belongs to a time when "poetry-novels" such as Byron's *Childe Harold* and Robert Bloomfield's *The Farmer's Boy* were popular reading, but yet must still be seen in its entirety.

For centuries personal tragedy—Henry Howard—and hardship—Ann Candler—would seem to have dominated Suffolk poets. But Aidan Semmens reminds us how rational and vigorous most of them were, realistically balancing light and darkness. Unexpectedly too we have Anna Barbauld's feisty *The Rights of Women* and *Washing Day*.

I read the anthology sitting outside under the roses with all the birds singing in their best Elizabethan (I) way, and feeling glad that someone had strewn all these poems together so knowledgeably. Some of the contemporary poems are quite wonderful—and a revelation to me. Even the familiar inclusions have gathered excitement.

Until almost within living memory Suffolk was a farming-fishing place, not all that far from London, yet strangely remote all the same. Its bright and often uncomfortable climate appeared to make artists and writers. As did its superb architecture and its huge band of sea. If Suffolk said one word it was "work".

And so here we have one man's choice of works great and small, a collected poetry from the past to the present. And all of it both contained and released, created in and by "Suffolk" to various extents, a true anthology, and one which is both a critique and a celebration of an extraordinarily inspiring area. It could not have been better chosen.

Introduction

Suffolk: England's easternmost county and also its driest—at least if you consider only rainfall. For Suffolk is in a sense defined by water: its rivers, each of which meanders gently, almost hidden among the fields and lanes, until suddenly widening into estuarial expanse, a broad coastal fraying of mudflats, tidal reaches and shifting islets, a territory of wading birds; the great bounding expanse of the grey North Sea; and most dramatically the erosive power of that sea, which has made of Covehithe church an imposing clifftop ruin, put that of Kessingland, once a mile inland, on the very edge of the beach, and most famously taken the once thriving medieval port city of Dunwich almost entirely under its waves. The eminent Victorian Algernon Charles Swinburne was not the first or last poet to be struck by the topography and the tale of Dunwich, his long poem from which this collection takes its title neither the first nor last to dramatise them. Equally popular with poets has been the town of Aldeburgh—the Borough of George Crabbe's wonderful sustained drama—which was already something of a haven for writers and artists before Benjamin Britten made it the base (at least nominally) for his annual music festival. In recent times, the nearby nuclear power station at Sizewell has also attracted poetic remark, as a few references in poems collected here attest.

Inland, Suffolk remains something of an enigma. It has no city, and for a few centuries until the parish church of St James at Bury St Edmunds—a long way from being the county's finest—was upgraded in 1914, it had no cathedral. In Suffolk today you are never far out of sight of a medieval church, a fact perhaps most noticeable to visitors and new arrivals to the county and closely related to its occasional title 'silly Suffolk', derived from the old word 'sylly' or 'sely', meaning 'holy'. No county in medieval England was syllier than Suffolk—though its rich heritage of church buildings owes more to its economic history than anything unique about the local degree of religious devotion. The joy of East Anglia is to have been the richest and, after London, the most populous area of England in the 150 years or so (1350-1500) when the building or re-building of parish churches was at its peak of both quantity and quality—and then to have fallen on relatively fallow times. The result is a rich heritage of wonderful buildings, rich in historic art, which, although suffering considerably the depredations of the Reformation and

Commonwealth periods, were relatively unaffected by the enthusiasms of later 'restorers' and 'improvers'.

As of today—and I say this with some trepidation for the future—Suffolk remains thankfully little 'improved'. No motorway intrudes on its rural calm. It is not on the way to anywhere—except for those containers of multifarious freight that pass through Felixstowe, which from a genteel seaside resort has been transformed, incongruously, into Britain's busiest port. Not that you would guess at that distinction from spending a day among the anglers on the stones of Landguard beach or just upriver in a hide watching the birdlife on the neighbouring wetland. And here we are, you see, drawn irresistibly again already back to the coast and the water, as the poets here almost always seem to be.

The earliest poet we can place confidently in Suffolk is John Lydgate, a close friend of Geoffrey Chaucer's son, and a monk at the Abbey of Bury St Edmunds. His verse is best known for its remarkable quantity. I decided, reluctantly, against giving him space in this volume partly because of his prolixity but more because 15th-century English, and 15th century concerns, are simply too far from our own to pass without either "translation" into modern idiom—which almost inevitably loses much of the flavour of the original as well as its authenticity—or copious explanatory footnotes, which would not fit well in an anthology of this kind.

After Lydgate comes Henry Howard who, though Earl of Surrey, was an East Anglian and is buried in the family church at Framlingham. The poems of his included here are not 'translated', though spelling and punctuation have been partly modernised in the manner common to modern editions of 16th-century works. A courtier at the court of Henry VIII, he suffered the same eventual fate as his kinswomen Anne Boleyn and Katherine Howard—a fate which also befell (metaphorically) Lydgate's old abbey, which might have become one of England's great cathedrals had its abbot's power not persuaded Henry to have it not merely dissolved but demolished, and (literally) another powerful Suffolk cleric, Thomas Wolsey. One can only speculate on how different Ipswich, and the county, might have been had Cardinal Wolsey lived to bring into being his dream of making of his home town a university city to rival Oxford and Cambridge: that the only relic of that scheme should be one brick gateway, badly eroded by fumes from the roadway it seems always in imminent danger of collapsing into, seems emblematic of Ipswich as it is today. The county town, strangely, has almost evaded poetic attention. Only one of the poets collected here (the youngest, and a native Ipswichian) appears to have noticed its existence.

The others have been drawn repeatedly to Suffolk's glorious medieval churches (notably, but by no means exclusively, R.F. Langley), to the rhythms of its agricultural year and, predominantly, to its unique and extraordinary coast, where—in the words of Britten's Peter Grimes, incised by sculptor Maggi Hambling in the justly famous sculpture on Aldeburgh beach commemorating Britten and pictured on the cover of this book—you might "hear those voices that will not be drowned".

The choice of those voices is mine; the impetus to make the selection came from John Matthias. It began with an email note in which he wrote: "I've been turning over in my mind the notion that someone should edit a book of poems re Suffolk of an unusual enough character that it could include you, me, R.F. Langley, Michael Hamburger, etc, but also poems by Crabbe and Swinburne." Who could resist such an implied invitation from perhaps the foremost living Suffolk poet (if a man born, raised and now again resident in the United States can be called a "Suffolk poet", which, for the purposes of this anthology, he obviously can)? So, with the support of Shearsman's Tony Frazer—John's publisher and mine—the process of putting this book together was soon under way. I hope in its completed form it is indeed of unusual enough character both to please John Matthias and to introduce a wide range of readers to work in a variety of modes they might not normally embrace. This has certainly been the case for me in researching the extraordinary number and variety of poets whose work qualifies for a "Suffolk" heading, either by being written by residents of the county, or by visitors placing their work within its landscape.

The most enjoyable aspect of the editing task has been discovering the great wealth of writing associated with Suffolk and immersing myself in poetry of many different kinds. The most difficult has been steeling myself to leave things out. I would very happily, for example, have republished all of R.F. Langley's *Collected Poems*—a slim volume which contains fewer words than the single poem of Robert Bloomfield's from which I have selected excerpts as judiciously as I could. Among the very few works I have been prevented from including for copyright reasons, I would encourage interested readers to seek out the final section, *Dark Night Sallies Forth*, from *After Nature*, Michael Hamburger's sensitive translation of a work by W.G. Sebald, a truly first-rate and perceptive prose writer whose rare venture into verse is a very welcome surprise;

and another translation, the extraordinary *Bixley Remedial School*, some of which is reprinted in *The Drug of Art, Selected Poems* by Ivan Blatný, a Czech modernist and surrealist who spent many of his later years as a mental patient at St Clement's Hospital in Ipswich, where many of his shortest and most gnomic poems were written. Those pleasures are for your discovery after the discoveries I hope you will make here—and perhaps after seeking out, as I hope you will, more work by those poets you enjoy in this book.

I won't attempt here a critical analysis of any of the poems I have chosen, but merely encourage each reader to give each writer the time and respect they all variously deserve—especially, perhaps, those they might not have sought out otherwise. Richard Caddel's introduction to the excellent 1999 anthology *Other: British and Irish Poetry since 1970* makes a clear and cogent distinction between what he calls "high street" poetry and the alternative kind(s) he preferred: I hope he would appreciate the attempt I have made to walk both streets, to pause on the corners between them, and to look out across Suffolk from both its highways and byways.

I am indebted to John Matthias not only for his original idea but especially for his support, encouragement and valuable suggestions throughout the process of putting the book together; to Tony Frazer for agreeing to publish it; to all those poets who have provided encouragement as well as poems; to all those publishers who have graciously allowed me to reprint work from existing volumes; and to Barbara Langley, Anne Beresford, Ann Caddel and Lucy Lomas, helpful and enthusiastic contributors to the process of selecting fitting work by their late husbands and father.

Aidan Semmens

Part I

A Suffolk Legacy

Algernon Charles Swinburne
(1837-1909)

From By the North Sea

Here, where sharp the sea-bird shrills his ditty,
Flickering flame-wise through the clear live calm,
Rose triumphal, crowning all a city,
Roofs exalted once with prayer and psalm,
Built of holy hands for holy pity,
Frank and fruitful as a sheltering palm.

Church and hospice wrought in faultless fashion,
Hall and chancel bounteous and sublime,
Wide and sweet and glorious as compassion,
Filled and thrilled with force of choral chime,
Filled with spirit of prayer and thrilled with passion,

Hailed a God more merciful than Time.
Ah, less mighty, less than Time prevailing,
Shrunk, expelled, made nothing at his nod,
Less than clouds across the sea-line sailing,
Lies he, stricken by his master's rod.

"Where is man?" the cloister murmurs wailing;
Back the mute shrine thunders—"Where is God?"
Here is all the end of all his glory—
Dust, and grass, and barren silent stones.
Dead, like him, one hollow tower and hoary

Naked in the sea-wind stands and moans,
Filled and thrilled with its perpetual story:
Here, where earth is dense with dead men's bones.
Low and loud and long, a voice for ever,
Sounds the wind's clear story like a song.

Tomb from tomb the waves devouring sever,
Dust from dust as years relapse along;
Graves where men made sure to rest, and never
Lie dismantled by the seasons' wrong.
Now displaced, devoured and desecrated,

Now by Time's hands darkly disinterred,
These poor dead that sleeping here awaited
Long the archangel's re-creating word,
Closed about with roofs and walls high-gated
Till the blast of judgment should be heard,

Naked, shamed, cast out of consecration,
Corpse and coffin, yea the very graves,
Scoffed at, scattered, shaken from their station,
Spurned and scourged of wind and sea like slaves,
Desolate beyond man's desolation,

Shrink and sink into the waste of waves.
Tombs, with bare white piteous bones protruded,
Shroudless, down the loose collapsing banks,
Crumble, from their constant place detruded,
That the sea devours and gives not thanks.

Graves where hope and prayer and sorrow brooded
Gape and slide and perish, ranks on ranks.
Rows on rows and line by line they crumble,
They that thought for all time through to be.
Scarce a stone whereon a child might stumble

Breaks the grim field paced alone of me.
Earth, and man, and all their gods wax humble
Here, where Time brings pasture to the sea.

Henry Howard, Earl of Surrey
(c1517-1547)

Description of Spring
Wherein every thing renews, save only the lover

The soote season, that bud and bloom forth brings,
With green hath clad the hill and eke the vale:
The nightingale with feathers new she sings:
The turtle to her mate hath told her tale:
Summer is come, for every spray now springs,
The hart hath hung his old head on the pale:
The buck in brake his winter coat he flings:
The fishes float with new repaired scale:
The adder all her slough away she slings:
The swift swallow pursueth the flies smale:
The busy bee her honey now she mings:
Winter is worn that was the flowers' bale.
    And thus I see among these pleasant things
    Each care decays, and yet my sorrow springs.

The Lover Comforteth Himself with the Worthiness of his Love

When raging love with extreme pain
Most cruelly distrains my heart:
When that my tears, as floods of rain,
Bear witness of my woeful smart:
When sighs have wasted so my breath
That I lie at the point of death:
I call to mind the navy great
That the Greeks brought to Troy town:
And how the boisterous winds did beat
Their ships, and rent their sails a-down;
Till Agamemnon's daughter's blood
Appeased the gods, that them withstood.
And how that in those ten years war
Full many a bloody deed was done,
And many a lord, that came full far,
There caught his bane (alas) too soon:
And many a good knight overrun,
Before the Greeks had Helen won.
Then think I thus: sith such repair,
So long time war of valiant men,
Was all to win a lady fair:
Shall I not learn to suffer then,
And think my life well spent to be,
Serving a worthier wight than she?
Therefore I never will repent,
But pains contented still endure.
For like as when, rough winter spent,
The pleasant spring straight draweth in ure:
So after raging storms of care
Joyful at length may be my fare.

A Complaint by Night

Alas so all things now do hold their peace.
Heaven and earth disturbed in nothing:
The beasts, the air, the birds their song do cease:
The night's chare the stars about doth bring.
Calm is the sea, the waves work less and less:
So am not I, whom love alas doth wring,
Bringing before my face the great increase
Of my desires, whereat I weep and sing,
In joy and woe, as in a doubtful ease.
For my sweet thoughts sometime do pleasure bring:
But by and by the cause of my disease
Gives me a pang, that inwardly doth sting,
    When that I think what grief it is again,
    To live and lack the thing should rid my pain.

Ann Candler
(1740-1814)

Reflections on My Own Situation

*Written in Tattingstone House of Industry,
February 1802*

How many years are past and gone,
    How alter'd I appear,
How many strange events have known,
    Since first I enter'd here!

Within these dreary walls confin'd,
    A lone recluse, I live,
And, with the dregs of human kind,
    A niggard alms receive.

Uncultivated, void of sense,
    Unsocial, insincere,
Their rude behaviour gives offence,
    Their language wounds the ear.

Disgusting objects swarm around,
    Throughout confusions reign;
Where feuds and discontent abound,
    Remonstrance proves in vain.

No sympathising friend I find,
    Unknown is friendship here;
Not one to soothe, or calm the mind,
    When overwhelm'd with care:

Peace, peace, my heart, thy duty calls,
    With cautious steps proceed:
Beyond these melancholy walls,
    I've found a friend indeed!

I gaze on numbers in distress,
    Compare their state with mine:
Can I reflect, and not confess
    A providence divine?

And I might bend beneath the rod,
    And equal want deplore,
But that a good and gracious God
    Is pleas'd to give me more:

My gen'rous friends, with feeling heart,
    Remove the pondrous weight,
And those impending ills avert
    Which want and woes create.

Yet what am I, that I should be
    Thus honor'd and carest?
And why such favors heap'd on me,
    And with such friendship blest?

Absorb'd in thought I often sate
    Within my lonely cell,
And mark'd the strange mysterious fate
    That seem'd to guide me still.

When keenest sorrow urg'd her claim,
    When evils threaten'd dread,
Some unexpected blessing came,
    And rais'd my drooping head.

In youth strange fairy tales I've read,
    Of magic skill and pow'r,
And mortals, in their sleep, convey'd
    To some enchanted tow'r.

In this obscure and lone retreat,
    Conceal'd from vulgar eyes,
Two rival genii us'd to meet
    And counterplots devise.

The evil genius, prone to ill,
    Mischievous schemes invents,
Pursues the fated mortal still,
    And ev'ry woe augments.

Insulted with indignant scorn,
    Aw'd by tyrannic sway,
A prey to grief each rising morn,
    And cheerless all the day.

But fate and fortune in their scenes
    A pleasing change decree:
The friendly genius intervenes,
    And sets the captive free.

Content and freedom thus regain'd,
    Depriv'd of both before;
So great the blessing, when obtain'd,
    What can he wish for more?

The tales these eastern writers feign
    Like facts to me appear;
The fabled suff'rings they contain,
    I find no fictions here.

And since, in those romantic lays,
    My miseries combine,
To bless my lengthen'd wane of days,
    Their bright reverse be mine.

Look down, O God! in me behold
    How helpless mortals are,
Nor leave me friendless, poor, and old,
    But guide me with thy care.

On the Birth of Twin Sons

In 1781

Hail, infant boys! and hail the dawn
    That brought your natal hour!
May no malignant planet frown
    With inauspicious pow'r.

May heav'n it's kindest influence shed
    Around ye as ye lay,
And watchful angels guard your bed,
    And shield ye in the day.

Sweet balmy slumbers close your eyes
    Whene'er dispos'd to rest;
Your waking, supplicating, cries,
    With pity move each breast.

On both may truth and goodness wait
    As they advance in age,
And may they find a milder fate
    Than what their births presage.

O, God! behold their infant state
    Thy kind protection claim:—
For them thy mercy I entreat;
    To me extend the same.

Tho', poor and helpless, I am here;
    On Thee my hopes rely;
Thou canst disperse the rising tear,
    And make me smile with joy.

O! give me, while thus mean and low,
    An humble peaceful mind,
May love and duty guide me through.
    With fortitude combin'd.

Could these dear boys their father's love,
    Join'd with their mother's, share,
How vast a blessing would it prove,
    How lighten ev'ry care!

What jarring sentiments contend
    And struggle, in my breast,
When I reflect they want the friend
    That should their youth assist!

O! peace, my soul, and be not griev'd;
    Repress each plaintive word;
And may these gifts, from heav'n receiv'd,
    Find favor with the Lord.

For them, for me, I humbly ask
    A portion of His grace,
And may we find, when life is past,
    With Him a resting place.

Anna Laetitia Barbauld
(1743-1825)

The Rights of Women

Yes, injured Woman! rise, assert thy right!
Woman! too long degraded, scorned, opprest;
O born to rule in partial Law's despite,
Resume thy native empire o'er the breast!

Go forth arrayed in panoply divine;
That angel pureness which admits no stain;
Go, bid proud Man his boasted rule resign,
And kiss the golden sceptre of thy reign.

Go, gird thyself with grace; collect thy store
Of bright artillery glancing from afar;
Soft melting tones thy thundering cannon's roar,
Blushes and fears thy magazine of war.

Thy rights are empire: urge no meaner claim,—
Felt, not defined, and if debated, lost;
Like sacred mysteries, which withheld from fame,
Shunning discussion, are revered the most.

Try all that wit and art suggest to bend
Of thy imperial foe the stubborn knee;
Make treacherous Man thy subject, not thy friend;
Thou mayst command, but never canst be free.

Awe the licentious, and restrain the rude;
Soften the sullen, clear the cloudy brow:
Be, more than princes' gifts, thy favours sued;—
She hazards all, who will the least allow.

But hope not, courted idol of mankind,
On this proud eminence secure to stay;

Subduing and subdued, thou soon shalt find
Thy coldness soften, and thy pride give way.

Then, then, abandon each ambitious thought,
Conquest or rule thy heart shall feebly move,
In Nature's school, by her soft maxims taught,
That separate rights are lost in mutual love.

Washing Day

The Muses are turned gossips; they have lost
The buskined step, and clear high-sounding phrase,
Language of gods. Come, then, domestic Muse,
In slip-shod measure loosely prattling on,
Of farm or orchard, pleasant curds and cream,
Or droning flies, or shoes lost in the mire
By little whimpering boy, with rueful face—
Come, Muse, and sing the dreaded washing day.
Ye who beneath the yoke of wedlock bend,
With bowed soul, full well ye ken the day
Which week, smooth sliding after week, brings on
Too soon; for to that day nor peace belongs,
Nor comfort; ere the first grey streak of dawn,
The red-armed washers come and chase repose.
Nor pleasant smile, nor quaint device of mirth,
Ere visited that day; the very cat,
From the wet kitchen scared, and reeking hearth,
Visits the parlour, an unwonted guest.
The silent breakfast meal is soon despatched,
Uninterrupted, save by anxious looks
Cast at the louring, if sky should lour.
From that last evil, oh preserve us, heavens!
For should the skies pour down, adieu to all
Remains of quiet; then expect to hear
Of sad disasters—dirt and gravel stains
Hard to efface, and loaded lines at once

Snapped short, and linen-horse by dog thrown down,
And all the petty miseries of life.
Saints have been calm while stretched upon the rack,
And Montezuma smiled on burning coals;
But never yet did housewife notable
Greet with a smile a rainy washing day.
But grant the welkin fair, require not thou
Who callest thyself, perchance, the master there,
Or study swept, or nicely dusted coat,
Or usual 'tendence; ask not, indiscreet,
Thy stockings mended, though the yawning rents
Gape wide as Erebus; nor hope to find
Some snug recess impervious. Shouldst thou try
The 'customed garden walks, thine eye shall rue
The budding fragrance of thy tender shrubs,
Myrtle or rose, all crushed beneath the weight
Of coarse-checked apron, with impatient hand
Twitched off when showers impend; or crossing lines
Shall mar thy musings, as the wet cold sheet
Flaps in thy face abrupt. Woe to the friend
Whose evil stars have urged him forth to claim
On such a day the hospitable rites;
Looks blank at best, and stinted courtesy
Shall he receive; vainly he feeds his hopes
With dinner of roast chicken, savoury pie,
Or tart or pudding; pudding he nor tart
That day shall eat; nor, though the husband try—
Mending what can't be helped—to kindle mirth
From cheer deficient, shall his consort's brow
Clear up propitious; the unlucky guest
In silence dines, and early slinks away.
I well remember, when a child, the awe
This day struck into me; for then the maids,
I scarce knew why, looked cross, and drove me from them;
Nor soft caress could I obtain, nor hope
Usual indulgencies; jelly or creams,
Relic of costly suppers, and set by
For me their petted one; or buttered toast,
When butter was forbid; or thrilling tale

Of ghost, or witch, or murder. So I went
And sheltered me beside the parlour fire;
There my dear grandmother, eldest of forms,
Tended the little ones, and watched from harm;
Anxiously fond, though oft her spectacles
With elfin cunning hid, and oft the pins
Drawn from her ravelled stocking, might have soured
One less indulgent.
At intervals my mother's voice was heard,
Urging dispatch; briskly the work went on,
All hands employed to wash, to rinse, to wring,
Or fold, and starch, and clap, and iron, and plait.
Then would I sit me down, and ponder much
Why washings were; sometimes through hollow hole
Of pipe amused we blew, and sent aloft
The floating bubbles; little dreaming then
To see, Montgolfier, thy silken ball
Ride buoyant through the clouds, so near approach
The sports of children and the toils of men.
Earth, air, and sky, and ocean hath its bubbles,
And verse is one of them—this most of all.

George Crabbe
(1754-1832)

Peter Grimes (The Borough, Letter XXII)

Old Peter Grimes made fishing his employ,
His wife he cabin'd with him and his boy,
And seem'd that life laborious to enjoy:
To town came quiet Peter with his fish,
And had of all a civil word and wish.
He left his trade upon the sabbath-day,
And took young Peter in his hand to pray:
But soon the stubborn boy from care broke loose,
At first refused, then added his abuse:
His father's love he scorn'd, his power defied,
But being drunk, wept sorely when he died.

Yes! then he wept, and to his mind there came
Much of his conduct, and he felt the shame,—
How he had oft the good old man reviled,
And never paid the duty of a child;
How, when the father in his Bible read,
He in contempt and anger left the shed:
"It is the word of life," the parent cried;
—"This is the life itself," the boy replied;
And while old Peter in amazement stood,
Gave the hot spirit to his boiling blood:—
How he, with oath and furious speech, began
To prove his freedom and assert the man;
And when the parent check'd his impious rage,
How he had cursed the tyranny of age,—
Nay, once had dealt the sacrilegious blow
On his bare head, and laid his parent low;
The father groan'd—"If thou art old," said he,
"And hast a son—thou wilt remember me:
Thy mother left me in a happy time,
Thou kill'dst not her—Heav'n spares the double-crime."

On an inn-settle, in his maudlin grief,
This he revolved, and drank for his relief.

Now lived the youth in freedom, but debarr'd
From constant pleasure, and he thought it hard;
Hard that he could not every wish obey,
But must awhile relinquish ale and play;
Hard! that he could not to his cards attend,
But must acquire the money he would spend.

With greedy eye he look'd on all he saw,
He knew not justice, and he laugh'd at law;
On all he mark'd he stretch'd his ready hand;
He fish'd by water, and he filch'd by land:
Oft in the night has Peter dropp'd his oar,
Fled from his boat and sought for prey on shore;
Oft up the hedge-row glided, on his back
Bearing the orchard's produce in a sack,
Or farm-yard load, tugg'd fiercely from the stack;
And as these wrongs to greater numbers rose,
The more he look'd on all men as his foes.

He built a mud-wall'd hovel, where he kept
His various wealth, and there he oft-times slept;
But no success could please his cruel soul,
He wish'd for one to trouble and control;
He wanted some obedient boy to stand
And bear the blow of his outrageous hand;
And hoped to find in some propitious hour
A feeling creature subject to his power.

Peter had heard there were in London then,—
Still have they being!—workhouse clearing men,
Who, undisturb'd by feelings just or kind,
Would parish-boys to needy tradesmen bind:
They in their want a trifling sum would take,
And toiling slaves of piteous orphans make.

Such Peter sought, and when a lad was found,
The sum was dealt him, and the slave was bound.

Some few in town observed in Peter's trap
A boy, with jacket blue and woollen cap;
But none inquired how Peter used the rope,
Or what the bruise, that made the stripling stoop;
None could the ridges on his back behold,
None sought his shiv'ring in the winter's cold;
None put the question,—"Peter, dost thou give
The boy his food?—What, man! the lad must live:
Consider, Peter, let the child have bread,
He'll serve thee better if he's stroked and fed."
None reason'd thus—and some, on hearing cries,
Said calmly, "Grimes is at his exercise."

Pinn'd, beaten, cold, pinch'd, threaten'd, and abused—
His efforts punish'd and his food refused,—
Awake tormented,—soon aroused from sleep,—
Struck if he wept, and yet compell'd to weep,
The trembling boy dropp'd down and strove to pray,
Received a blow, and trembling turn'd away,
Or sobb'd and hid his piteous face;—while he,
The savage master, grinn'd in horrid glee:
He'd now the power he ever loved to show,
A feeling being subject to his blow.

Thus lived the lad, in hunger, peril, pain,
His tears despised, his supplications vain:
Compell'd by fear to lie, by need to steal,
His bed uneasy and unbless'd his meal,
For three sad years the boy his tortures bore,
And then his pains and trials were no more.

"How died he, Peter?" when the people said,
He growl'd—"I found him lifeless in his bed;"
Then tried for softer tone, and sigh'd, "Poor Sam is dead."
Yet murmurs were there, and some questions ask'd,—
How he was fed, how punish'd, and how task'd?
Much they suspected, but they little proved,
And Peter pass'd untroubled and unmoved.

Another boy with equal ease was found,
The money granted, and the victim bound;
And what his fate?—One night it chanced he fell
From the boat's mast and perish'd in her well.
Where fish were living kept, and where the boy
(So reason'd men) could not himself destroy:—

"Yes! so it was," said Peter, "in his play,
(For he was idle both by night and day,)
He climb'd the main-mast and then fell below;"—
Then show'd his corpse and pointed to the blow:
"What said the jury?"—they were long in doubt,
But sturdy Peter faced the matter out:
So they dismiss'd him, saying at the time,
"Keep fast your hatchway when you've boys who climb."
This hit the conscience, and he colour'd more
Than for the closest questions put before.

Thus all his fears the verdict set aside,
And at the slave-shop Peter still applied.

Then came a boy, of manners soft and mild,—
Our seamen's wives with grief beheld the child;
All thought (the poor themselves) that he was one
Of gentle blood, some noble sinner's son,
Who had, belike, deceived some humble maid,
Whom he had first seduced and then betray'd:
However this, he seem'd a gracious lad,
In grief submissive and with patience sad.

Passive he labour'd, till his slender frame
Bent with his loads, and he at length was lame:
Strange that a frame so weak could bear so long
The grossest insult and the foulest wrong;
But there were causes—in the town they gave
Fire, food, and comfort, to the gentle slave;
And though stern Peter, with a cruel hand,
And knotted rope, enforced the rude command,
Yet he considered what he'd lately felt,
And his vile blows with selfish pity dealt.

One day such draughts the cruel fisher made,
He could not vend them in his borough-trade,
But sail'd for London-mart: the boy was ill,
But ever humbled to his master's will;
And on the river, where they smoothly sail'd,
He strove with terror and awhile prevail'd;
But new to danger on the angry sea,
He clung affrighten'd to his master's knee:
The boat grew leaky and the wind was strong,
Rough was the passage and the time was long;
His liquor fail'd, and Peter's wrath arose,—
No more is known—the rest we must suppose,
Or learn of Peter;—Peter says, he "spied
The stripling's danger and for harbour tried;
Meantime the fish, and then th' apprentice died."

The pitying women raised a clamour round,
And weeping said, "Thou hast thy 'prentice drown'd."

Now the stern man was summon'd to the hall,
To tell his tale before the burghers all:
He gave th' account; profess'd the lad he loved,
And kept his brazen features all unmoved.

The mayor himself with tone severe replied,
"Henceforth with thee shall never boy abide;
Hire thee a freeman, whom thou durst not beat,
But who, in thy despite, will sleep and eat:
Free thou art now!—again shouldst thou appear,
Thou'lt find thy sentence, like thy soul, severe."

Alas! for Peter not a helping hand,
So was he hated, could he now command;
Alone he row'd his boat, alone he cast
His nets beside, or made his anchor fast;
To hold a rope or hear a curse was none,—
He toil'd and rail'd; he groan'd and swore alone.

Thus by himself compell'd to live each day,
To wait for certain hours the tide's delay;

At the same times the same dull views to see,
The bounding marsh-bank and the blighted tree;
The water only, when the tides were high,
When low, the mud half-cover'd and half-dry;
The sun-burnt tar that blisters on the planks,
And bank-side stakes in their uneven ranks;
Heaps of entangled weeds that slowly float,
As the tide rolls by the impeded boat.

When tides were neap, and, in the sultry day,
Through the tall bounding mud-banks made their way,
Which on each side rose swelling, and below
The dark warm flood ran silently and slow;
There anchoring, Peter chose from man to hide,
There hang his head, and view the lazy tide
In its hot slimy channel slowly glide;
Where the small eels that left the deeper way
For the warm shore, within the shallows play;
Where gaping mussels, left upon the mud,
Slope their slow passage to the fallen flood;—
Here dull and hopeless he'd lie down and trace
How sidelong crabs had scrawl'd their crooked race;

Or sadly listen to the tuneless cry
Of fishing gull or clanging golden-eye;
What time the sea-birds to the marsh would come,
And the loud bittern, from the bulrush home,
Gave from the salt-ditch side the bellowing boom:
He nursed the feelings these dull scenes produce,
And loved to stop beside the opening sluice;
Where the small stream, confined in narrow bound,
Ran with a dull, unvaried, sadd'ning sound;
Where all, presented to the eye or ear,
Oppress'd the soul with misery, grief, and fear.

Besides these objects, there were places three,
Which Peter seem'd with certain dread to see;
When he drew near them he would turn from each,
And loudly whistle till he pass'd the reach.

A change of scene to him brought no relief;
In town, 'twas plain, men took him for a thief:
The sailors' wives would stop him in the street,
And say, "Now, Peter, thou'st no boy to beat":
Infants at play, when they perceived him, ran,
Warning each other—"That's the wicked man":
He growl'd an oath, and in an angry tone
Cursed the whole place and wish'd to be alone.

Alone he was, the same dull scenes in view,
And still more gloomy in his sight they grew:
Though man he hated, yet employ'd alone
At bootless labour, he would swear and groan,
Cursing the shoals that glided by the spot,
And gulls that caught them when his arts could not.

Cold nervous tremblings shook his sturdy frame,
And strange disease—he couldn't say the name;
Wild were his dreams, and oft he rose in fright,
Waked by his view of horrors in the night,—
Horrors that would the sternest minds amaze,
Horrors that demons might be proud to raise:
And though he felt forsaken, grieved at heart,
To think he lived from all mankind apart;
Yet, if a man approach'd, in terrors he would start.

A winter pass'd since Peter saw the town,
And summer-lodgers were again come down;
These, idly curious, with their glasses spied
The ships in bay as anchor'd for the tide,—
The river's craft,—the bustle of the quay, –
And sea-port views, which landmen love to see.

One, up the river, had a man and boat
Seen day by day, now anchor'd, now afloat;
Fisher he seemed, yet used no net nor hook;
Of sea-fowl swimming by no heed he took,
But on the gliding waves still fix'd his lazy look:
At certain stations he would view the stream,

As if he stood bewilder'd in a dream,
Or that some power had chain'd him for a time,
To feel a curse or meditate on crime.

This known, some curious, some in pity went,
And others question'd—"Wretch, dost thou repent?"
He heard, he trembled, and in fear resign'd
His boat: new terror fill'd his restless mind;
Furious he grew, and up the country ran,
And there they seized him—a distemper'd man:—
Him we received, and to a parish-bed,
Follow'd and curs'd, the groaning man was led.

Here when they saw him, whom they used to shun,
A lost, lone man, so harass'd and undone;
Our gentle females, ever prompt to feel,
Perceived compassion on their anger steal;
His crimes they could not from their memories blot,
But they were grieved, and trembled at his lot.

A priest too came, to whom his words are told
And all the signs they shudder'd to behold.

"Look! look!" they cried; "his limbs with horror shake.
And as he grinds his teeth, what noise they make!
How glare his angry eyes, and yet he's not awake:
See! what cold drops upon his forehead stand,
And how he clenches that broad bony hand."

The priest attending, found he spoke at times
As one alluding to his fears and crimes:
"It was the fall," he mutter'd, "I can show
The manner how—I never struck a blow":—
And then aloud—"Unhand me, free my chain;
An oath, he fell—it struck him to the brain:—
Why ask my father?—that old man will swear
Against my life; besides, he wasn't there:—
What, all agreed?—Am I to die to-day?—
My Lord, in mercy, give me time to pray."

Then, as they watch'd him, calmer he became,
And grew so weak he couldn't move his frame,
But murmuring spake,—while they could see and hear
The start of terror and the groan of fear;
See the large dew-beads on his forehead rise,
And the cold death-drop glaze his sunken eyes;
Nor yet he died, but with unwonted force
Seem'd with some fancied being to discourse:
He knew not us, or with accustom'd art
He hid the knowledge, yet exposed his heart;
'Twas part confession, and the rest defence,
A madman's tale, with gleams of waking sense.

"I'll tell you all," he said, "the very day
When the old man first placed them in my way:
My father's spirit—he who always tried
To give me trouble, when he lived and died—
When he was gone, he could not be content
To see my days in painful labour spent,
But would appoint his meetings, and he made
Me watch at these, and so neglect my trade.

"'Twas one hot noon, all silent, still, serene,
No living being had I lately seen;
I paddled up and down and dipp'd my net,
But (such his pleasure) I could nothing get,—
A father's pleasure, when his toil was done,
To plague and torture thus an only son!
And so I sat and look'd upon the stream,
How it ran on, and felt as in a dream:
But dream it was not: no!—I fix'd my eyes
On the mid stream and saw the spirits rise,
I saw my father on the water stand,
And hold a thin pale boy in either hand;
And there they glided ghastly on the top
Of the salt flood, and never touch'd a drop:
I would have struck them, but they knew th' intent,
And smiled upon the oar, and down they went.

"Now, from that day, whenever I began
To dip my net, there stood the hard old man—
He and those boys: I humbled me and pray'd
They would be gone;—they heeded not, but stay'd;
Nor could I turn, nor would the boat go by,
But gazing on the spirits, there was I:
They bade me leap to death, but I was loth to die:
And every day, as sure as day arose,
Would these three spirits meet me ere the close;
To hear and mark them daily was my doom,
And 'Come' they said, with weak, sad voices, 'come'.
To row away with all my strength I tried,
But there were they, hard by me in the tide,
The three unbodied forms—and 'Come', still 'come', they cried.

"Fathers should pity—but this old man shook
His hoary locks, and froze me by a look:
Thrice, when I struck them, through the water came
A hollow groan, that weaken'd all my frame:
'Father!' said I, 'have mercy':—He replied,
I know not what—the angry spirit lied,—
'Didst thou not draw thy knife?' said he:—
'Twas true, But I had pity and my arm withdrew:
He cried for mercy which I kindly gave,
But he has no compassion in his grave.

"There were three places, where they ever rose,—
The whole long river has not such as those,—
Places accursed, where, if a man remain,
He'll see the things which strike him to the brain;
And there they made me on my paddle lean,
And look at them for hours;—accursed scene!
When they would glide to that smooth eddy-space,
Then bid me leap and join them in the place;
And at my groans each little villain sprite
Enjoy'd my pains and vanish'd in delight.

"In one fierce summer-day, when my poor brain
Was burning hot, and cruel was my pain,
Then came this father-foe, and there he stood

With his two boys again upon the flood;
There was more mischief in their eyes, more glee
In their pale faces when they glared at me:
Still did they force me on the oar to rest,
And when they saw me fainting and oppress'd,
He, with his hand, the old man, scoop'd the flood,
And there came flame about him mix'd with blood;
He bade me stoop and look upon the place,
Then flung the hot-red liquor in my face;
Burning it blazed, and then I roar'd for pain,
I thought the demons would have turn'd my brain.

"Still there they stood, and forced me to behold
A place of horrors—they cannot be told—
Where the flood open'd, there I heard the shriek
Of tortured guilt—no earthly tongue can speak:
'All days alike! for ever!' did they say,
'And unremitted torments every day'—
Yes, so they said":—But here he ceased and gazed
On all around, affrighten'd and amazed;
And still he tried to speak, and look'd in dread
Of frighten'd females gathering round his bed;
Then dropp'd exhausted, and appear'd at rest,
Till the strong foe the vital powers possess'd:
Then with an inward, broken voice he cried,
"Again they come," and mutter'd as he died.

Robert Bloomfield
(1766-1823)

selections from The Farmer's Boy

from Spring

Where noble GRAFTON spreads his rich domains,
Round *Euston's* water'd vale, and sloping plains,
Where woods and groves in solemn grandeur rise,
Where the kite brooding unmolested flies;
The woodcock and the painted pheasant race,
And sculking foxes, destin'd for the chace;
There Giles, untaught and unrepining, stray'd
Thro' every copse, and grove, and winding glade;
There his first thoughts to Nature's charms inclin'd,
That stamps devotion on th' inquiring mind.
A little farm his generous Master till'd,
Who with peculiar grace his station fill'd;
By deeds of hospitality endear'd,
Serv'd from affection, for his worth rever'd;
A happy offspring blest his plenteous board,
His fields were fruitful, and his harm well stor'd,
And fourscore ewes he fed, a sturdy team,
And lowing kine that grazed beside the stream:
Unceasing industry he kept in view;
And never lack'd a job for Giles to do.

FLED now the sullen murmurs of the North,
The splendid raiment of the SPRING peeps forth;
Her universal green, and the clear sky,
Delight still more and more the gazing eye.
Wide o'er the fields, in rising moisture strong,
Shoots up the simple flower, or creeps along
The mellow'd soil; imbibing fairer hues
Or sweets from frequent showers and evening dews;
That summon from its shed the slumb'ring ploughs,

While health impregnates every breeze that blows.
No wheels support the diving pointed share;
No groaning ox is doom'd to labour there;
No helpmates teach the docile steed his road;
(Alike unknown the plow-boy and the goad;)
But, unassisted through each toilsome day,
With smiling brow the plowman cleaves his way,
Draws his fresh parallels, and wid'ning still,
Treads slow the heavy dale, or climbs the hill:
Strong on the wing his busy followers play,
Where writhing earth-worms meet th' unwelcome day;
Till all is chang'd, and hill and level down
Assume a livery of sober brown:
Again disturb'd, when Giles with wearying strides
From ridge to ridge the ponderous harrow guides;
His heels deep sinking every step he goes,
Till dirt usurp the empire of his shoes.
Welcome green headland! firm beneath his feet;
Welcome the friendly bank's refreshing seat;
There, warm with toil, his panting horses browse
Their shelt'ring canopy of pendent boughs;
Till rest, delicious, chase each transient pain,
And new-born vigour swell in every vein.
Hour after hour, and day to day succeeds;
Till every clod and deep-drawn furrow spreads
To crumbling mould; a level surface clear,
And strew'd with corn to crown the rising year;
And o'er the whole Giles once transverse again,
In earth's moist bosom buries up the grain.
The work is done; no more to man is given;
The grateful farmer trusts the rest to Heaven.
Yet oft with anxious heart he looks around,
And marks the first green blade that breaks the ground;
In fancy sees his trembling oats uprun,
His tufted barley yellow with the sun;
Sees clouds propitious shed their timely store,
And all his harvest gather'd round his door.
But still unsafe the big swoln grain below,
A fav'rite morsel with the Rook and Crow;

From field to field the flock increasing goes;
To level crops most formidable foes:
Their danger well the wary plunderers know,
And place a watch on some conspicuous bough;
Yet oft the sculking gunner by surprise
Will scatter death amongst them as they rise.
These, hung in triumph round the spacious field,
At best will but a short-lived terror yield:
Nor guards of property; (not penal law,
But harmless riflemen of rags and straw);
Familiariz'd to these, they boldly rove,
Nor heed such centinels that never move.
Let then your birds lie prostrate on the earth,
In dying posture, and with wings stretch'd forth;
Shift them at eve or morn from place to place,
And death shall terrify the pilfering race;
In the mid air, while circling round and round,
They call their lifeless comrades from the ground;
With quick'ning wing, and notes of loud alarm,
Warn the whole flock to shun the' impending harm.

This task had *Giles*, in fields remote from home:
Oft has he wish'd the rosy morn to come.
Yet never fam'd was he nor foremost found
To break the seal of sleep; his sleep was sound:
But when at day-break summon'd from his bed,
Light as the lark that carol'd o'er his head,
His sandy way deep-worn by hasty showers,
O'er-arch'd with oaks that form'd fantastic bow'rs,
Waving aloft their tow'ring branches proud,
In borrow'd tinges from the eastern cloud,
(Whence inspiration, pure as ever flow'd,
And genuine transport in his bosom glow'd)
His own shrill matin join'd the various notes
Of Nature's music, from a thousand throats:
The blackbird strove with emulation sweet,
And Echo answer'd from her close retreat;
The sporting white-throat on some twig's end borne,
Pour'd hymns to freedom and the rising morn;

Stopt in her song perchance the starting thrush
Shook a white shower from the black-thorn bush,
Where dew-drops thick as early blossoms hung,
And trembled as the minstrel sweetly sung.
Across his path, in either grove to hide,
The timid rabbit scouted by his side;
Or bold cock-pheasant stalk'd along the road,
Whose gold and purple tints alternate glow'd.
But groves no farther fenc'd the devious way;
A wide-extended heath before him lay,
Where on the grass the stagnant shower had run,
And shone a mirror to the rising sun,
(Thus doubly seen) lighting a distant wood,
Giving new life to each expanding bud;
Effacing quick the dewy foot-marks found,
Where prowling Reynard trod his nightly round;
To shun whose thefts 'twas Giles's evening care,
His feather'd victims to suspend in air,
High on the bough that nodded o'er his head,
And thus each morn to strew the field with dead.
His simple errand done, he homeward hies;
Another instantly its place supplies.
The clatt'ring dairy-maid immers'd in steam,
Singing and scrubbing midst her milk and cream,
Bawls out, *"Go fetch the cows…"*

from Autumn

The plough moves heavily, and strong the soil,
And clogging harrows with augmented toil
Dive deep: and clinging mixes with the mould
A fat'ning treasure from the nightly fold,
And all the cow-yard's highly valu'd store,
That late bestrew'd the blacken'd surface o'er.
No idling hours are here, when Fancy trims
Her dancing taper over outstretch'd limbs,
And in her thousand thousand colours drest,

Plays round the grassy couch of noontide rest:
Here GILES for hours of indolence atones
With strong exertion, and with weary bones,
And knows no leisure; till the distant chime
Of Sabbath bells he hears at sermon time,
That down the brook sound sweetly in the gale,
Or strike the rising hill, or skim the dale.

Nor his alone the sweets of ease to taste:
Kind rest extends to all;... save one poor beast,
That true to time and pace, is doom'd to plod,
To bring the Pastor to the HOUSE of GOD:
Mean structure; where no bones of heroes lie!
The rude inelegance of poverty
Reigns here alone: else why that roof of straw?
Those narrow windows with the frequent flaw?
O'er whose low cells the dock and mallow spread,
And rampant nettles lift the spiry head,
Whilst from the hollows of the tower on high
The grey-cap'd daws in saucy legions fly.

Round these lone walls assembling neighbours meet,
And tread departed friends beneath their feet;
And new-brier'd graves, that prompt the secret sigh,
Shew each the spot where he himself must lie.
Midst timely greetings village news goes round,
Of crops late shorn, or crops that deck the ground;
Experienc'd ploughmen in the circle join;
While sturdy boys, in feats of strength to shine,
With pride elate their young associates brave
To jump from hollow-sounding grave to grave;
Then close consulting, each his talent lends
To plan fresh sports when tedious service ends.

Bernard Barton
(1784-1849)

Dunwich

In Britain's earlier annals thou wert set
  Among the cities of our sea-girt isle:
Of what thou wert—some tokens linger yet
  In yonder ruins; and this roofless pile,
Whose walls are worshipless, whose tower—a mark,
Left but to guide the seaman's wandering bark!

Yet where those ruins grey are scatter'd round,
  The din of commerce fill'd the echoing air;
From these now crumbling walls arose the sound
  Of hallow'd music, and the voice of prayer;
And *this* was unto some, whose names have ceased,
The wall'd and gated City of the East!

Thus time, and circumstance, and change, betray
  The transient tenure of the worldly wise!
Thus "Trade's proud empire hastes to swift decay,"
  And leaves no splendid wreck for fame to prize.
While nature her magnificence retains,
And from the contrast added glory gains.

Still in its billowy boundlessness outspread,
  Yon mighty deep smiles to the orb of day,
Whose brightness o'er this shatter'd pile is shed
  In quiet beauty.—Nature's ancient sway
Is audible in winds that whisper round,
The soaring sky-lark's song, the breaker's hollow sound.

Part II

Recent and contemporary poets

Andy Brown

At Sizewell

A sign painter put the phrase up here in jest:
Zero Weather. Now, none but depressives
sun themselves on the shingle; their ration
of bravado squatting like a leathery old man
beside his bored grandsons. The beach itself
can manage no more than a crawl to the surf.
We knit arms under the elephant sky.
Reluctant to remain, you point to the horizon:
"This place is neither dead nor alive," you wheeze.
With the exception of some fast departing geese
no signs can prove you wrong, save out at sea
the phosphorescent streak astern a North Sea ferry
catching the eye and—if you look just hard enough—
a pod of sea-monsters breaking the green of the waves.

Merman

Beyond the Ness the fish-hands haul in nets.
Bald, with ragged beard and seal-skin naked,
some say the *thing* can shed his tail at will;
on land appears as all but human. The gillies
hand him over to the Governor, whose questions
he deflects in tongues of Cod and Plaice. In church
he shows no signs of Christian reverence.
They hang him by his feet and beat him senseless
with withies. He bears their torture silently,
eats nothing but Rollmop and Oyster,
month on month, preserving his wildness until,
lonely for his kind, he breaks away to sea,
flicking out the razor of his tail
to scythe across their fields of creels and nets.

Pine trees at Five Ways

The morning emerges in a counterpoint
of sun and mist;
                a day streaming into
their branches.
                    They stand rooted
into the vertical,
like a Giacometti string quartet
talking things over musically
in a deep shaft filled with light.

On my hand your fingers;
on your face my eyes,
our tongues silent
in the vacuum
                of a Sunday walk;

the spaces our bodies inhabit
defining spare geometries,
like the ring of the bells
in empty towers
                from here to Iken Marsh.

On the brow of a rise,
the pilots of two stunt kites
hang their souls on hooks of air.

From the edge of the mere,
the morning calls of unseen creatures
like oboe players lost in the reeds.

For a moment it's no longer clear
who is walking towards whom;
                        us, or the trees?

Angela Leighton

Scallop

for Maggi Hambling

In words the sky looks through, this thing
assigns the wind to its carved tune.

Striations of steel, the colour of nothing,
rib the altering wash of the sea.

Far off, you'd think: the fuselage
of a fallen angel, close to,

a cracked valve hemmed with letters.
It's wavy, flexed to filter wavelengths,

instrumental to onsets of weather,
literal in the palate of the wind.

Fantail, vaulting, locket or shell,
it opens like a listening muscle,

as if a phone or ear had sprung
on the grey shingle, set to listen.

Read, if you can, the sky in stencil,
touch the fluted hardware of a song,

something, not music, yet most musical,
fills this pleated clef of the sea,

this piece in steelwork full of whispers.
Nearer, trace the cut of its sound,

the speaking hollow of its beaten words—
an ear to its shape, an eye to its call:

"I hear those voices that will not be drowned."

Station

Dilatory ghosts of thistledown float and stick.
An empty platform steps off its own stage.
Two probes, divining rods, run on and on
in the curve of the world, silver under the sun.

Each knuckling bolt keeps crosswise sleepers down.
Saxifrage, stonecrop, those chivvying crickets,
swifts, like switchback racers, heaven's rivets,
cry, cry—a call at breaking pitch.

There are stations of the way no place-names nominate.
Nothing except what is here: high summer, weather,
chalk-white rubble underlining the way—
and we, in the wings of leaving with leave to wait,

stay for a while daydreaming indefinite stays.
Then a click, points-change, and the tiniest humming sets
the metal on edge, tunes its nerve, and rings
a steel cue in the ear: departure begins.

Tamar Yoseloff

The Butley Ferry (off season)

A rowboat marooned in the mud until Spring,
its prow thrusts towards the opposite shore,
shallows spotted with oystercatchers
teetering on red stilts, terns, and we turn

towards an indifferent sky—hard to tell
what season we are in—the colour of the mud
that wants to hold us in its grasp. Nothing to stop us
from ferrying ourselves across;

the trusting boatman has left the oars
folded like waiting arms inside his boat.
Beyond the riverbank the Ness
stretches a thumb across Orford Harbour,

silent now, its unexploded bombs
patient beneath the frozen ground,
the Pagodas like foreign girls who breeze
through town in summer; and beyond, the sea.

But the water is so black, the wind is picking up;
not a day to make a journey, not even
to the other side. We turn back, retrace our steps
to the last field. The bullocks watch us,

swaying on their skinny legs, their long babyfaces
so serious, chewing on hard grass, chewing,
their eyes like chunks of obsidian,
precious and cold.

The Muntjac

reflects our headlights in his eyes;
his scrubby body disappears into the hedge

now white with May,
tar and fern on his delicate hooves

and all at once the road reverts
to emptiness, but something of his presence

stays, an apparition on the verge:
fugitive from walled estates that favoured

curiosities, alien tropics *quick and rank*,
snaking beyond the boundaries, laying roots.

The road curves past Darks Dale floodlit,
a tractor ploughing furrows, past New Broke Ups,

Wrong Land; and beyond, a tangle of forest,
oaks hunched like old men against the night.

Ronald Blythe

Down to the Dwelling House

Steps from the B-road to the unlettered track
Return me daily to my Dwelling House,
As the deeds proclaim it.
Carts, herds and farming feet have impacted this flint mile.
Grass the height of axletrees has spared its crown.

I tread the grass to subdue this crown,
To stay it from doing more than it does,
Which is to stroke the bellies of cars.
My slight levelling might just save
A slicing of their exhaustive parts.

Intending guests telephone to ask,
Not, "How are you?" but "How is the track?"
All over England comes the question,
"How is your track?" It is most enquired of.
I consider then its metal, its middle rising proud,
And answer, "Fine." And indeed it is, most fine,
Most serviceable for its early intention,
Which was to carry farming feet, carts
And herds down to the Dwelling House.

But how is the track for Saabs and Minis,
Fiats even? This is what my guests are asking,
Though too polite to be that explicit.
I hear them rumbling away with low clearance
And self concern. Is it possible they might
Walk an uninitialled mile
From a B-road to a Dwelling House?

Take today, the Annunciation,
I tread the crown whilst fetching milk,
Ever thoughtful of these riders.

I see the cold stream pastures shining,
The corn hill pressing against the sky,
The March plants making cushions,
Black medick, agrimony, chervil, nettle,
Of course, all the new unravelling leaf.
Flower and wheat on the move.
I hear the wind answering the wires, feel

The track thinking back to what farming feet
Asked of it. Rough walkers on rough ground
Who trod it without assurances.

My Inland Gulls

Walking with yellow feet the slanting crests
And gleaming lacerations of the plough,
Screaming their salty platitudes, distracted,
Lost, testing their landed pinions in bursts of flight,
Demented, but with fierce eyes conning the
Strange field which, greening, races on
In unrelenting rows and parallels until
Its corrugations hit the sky,
A bird blizzard deletes the ploughman shares and all.
Homing down like diptych angels in loud succession
From above, for a while they struggled for a footing
Here on earth. Then fed, still shouting, it is,
"Which way to the sea?" But the fields rule on forever.

Victor Tapner

Sayer

The hearth is hushed

strange faces in firelight

men rest against the wattle walls
ale weary
their bellies heavy with feasting

To them
who see no farther than their fields
the same trees leafing in spring

my head is full of treasure
my mouth rich with gemstones

I'm a sharpened axe on an enemy's neck
an arrow singing in sunlight
a sword's arc in the wooded night

I earn the first meat from the flesh hook
the best bed in the round house

I trade with my tongue

a thatcher of stories
farmer of words

Homestead to homestead
I walk the sky's edge

an ear to the river's chatter

the kestrel's cry

the sighs of fenland trees
crippled in the wind

Iceni

With the first frosts the first death came
his face hair showed he was wasting

We drank those nights rank barley
from a cask and the lad drank too

He was with us when we caught
the moorhen and the goose

Then the wind cut like flint across the fen
and split the wattles of the round house

These marshes will bear a dark harvest
before spring comes and the corn

Shrill Water

Brown fish

brown
as river stones

fin flickering
eye watching
gills lifting
head
to the
cold flow

my spear tip
waits

to make
your
water
s
c
r
e
a
m

Pauline Stainer

Little Egypt[1]

1 *Sandpeople*

These are the sandpeople—
fixed by fugitive stain
in the acidic soil;
rayographs
on light-sensitive ground,
the real become the sign.

When we divested them
they lay north-south
in pagan burial;
encaustic, exemplary,
preparatory drawings
in silverpoint;

their insufficiency of bone
fluorescing
under ultra-violet,
an amber inclusion
still hung
at the striation of the throat.

No excavation
catches the slenderness
of their chance melting;
taking the first cast
we remembered those
from Pompeii

---

[1] *Little Egypt* is a local name for Sutton Hoo, the Anglo-Saxon burial-boat site in Suffolk, as well as a name sometimes given to the Orkney island of Rousay, which has many early tombs.

but later
seeing the half-profile
in fibreglass,
felt only
bright sufficiency
outstripping the bone.

2 Tide-mill near Sutton Hoo

It wasn't the pull of the tide I felt,
but the pull of men
raising the funeral-ship on the far shore;

how they hauled the clinker-built boat
over the red crag
up through the bracken;

sited it stern seawards
on the spur,
sank the gunwale below the barrow.

Such cold inlay—
only armourers on an enamel field
to fix the dye in the heart.

But then the tide turned, the sluice opened,
the medieval mill-wheels ground
as they had for the Black Canons

and looking out across the flood,
I remembered the inventory
of the sacrificial vessel:

bronze stag, stone sceptre,
baptismal silver
for the blood thickening inshore—

and I sensed how they crossed—
kingship,
the occurrence of mercy

and that bright error of judgement
which made the Saxon bird
flash through the lighted hall.

3 *Little Egypt*

Here in wartime,
army recruits packed
the excavated ship with bracken,
drove a glider trench
between the barrows

oblivious of
the tilt of the burial-boat
in the battle-ditch,
the king pillowed
amidship
between the tholes of the gunwale.

Weapons furnish sacrifice;
those who forged the rivets
for the ribbed hull,
left vizor and neck-guard,
sword and helmet,
cheekpieces of iron.

Now American planes
rise and fall
above the spur of the land,
whilst far below
where the estuary widens
the tide—gunmetal grey—
rises in the reeds.

4 *The Dig*

They map out the mound
like surgeons
dividing a belly,
scan for echoes.

Here the stern
of the burial-boat
was removed by ploughing.

On this female grave,
they uncover the goosewing
with which she swept out the oven;
the worn spiral
of an ammonite
where her dress
once opened at the breast.

It is quirkish of time
to leave only a purposeful echo
among the erratics:

this male body
buried in ploughing-position
beside his plough,
the eager figure
bent forward over the coulter—
fragile, passionate,
as if still reining-in
the light.

5 *Iken*

It was here
they broke the ground
for the burial of a stranger;

gave him
high above the estuary
a silent riding at anchor.

In the roofless nave
where the floor is shingle,
only baptism troubles the water;

on the chancel altar
a bleeding-bowl
of alluvial silver.

Nothing furnishes us
for such ebbs
of extraordinary fall—

for whether the miraculous
draught of fishes
is water or light

for the angel
figured on the luminous strand
with instruments of passion.

The bright source
of sacrament
is the dispossession of wounds;

how piercing-strange
the severity of the rite,
the inconsequence of the tide.

Lepers at Dunwich

Distance is different here—
between dissolvings—
dust fine as pouncing rosin
under the fresco
where the angels have lost their sandals

do not look at the lepers
but the spaces between—
the phrasing of spray
against sandstone,
martins mining the undercliff

attrition is
iodine on the wind,
the hairline eroded,
no purchase for the compass-point
to swing its halo

immunity
to ravish the unlovely—
even without lips
they are brides
of Christ

and he holds them
indissoluble
in the salt undertow
as if after the first drowning
there were no other.

John Matthias

Kedging

        's all you're good for
someone said. Is what? Your good

and for it. Not to fear: O all your
goods so far. Your good 4.

Your goods 5 and 6. With a little tug
at warp. So by a hawser winde

your head about. Thirty nine
among the sands your steps or

riddle there. Who may have
sailed the Alde is old now, olde

and addled, angling still for some
good luck. So labor, lad: *when other*

moiety of men, tugging hard at kedge
and hawser, drew us from

the sand? Brisk and lively in the
dialect East Anglian. *Ain't so well*

as I was yesterday, for I was then
quite kedge. Even though I pull and

pole and persevere I'm blown to
windward. Winding still. Warping so

as not to weep, cadging as I can.

Rivers

I

By touch: his twig reveals the waters,
his sounding rod bites into chalk.
Matrona, Bel and Wandil gather in the mist

upon the hillside, lean into the journey:
moon by sun against the darkness,
sun by moon against the giant with a sword.

By air: the signal from the Gogmagogs
to zodiacs at Edmund's Bury and Nuthampstead.
Knight to knight come forth. By air

the still response: the bull, the lion;
the eagle & the bear. If Wandil stole the spring,
spread his frost along the ley lines,

now he strides as Gemini across the sky.
(Not two children, not two goats,
but eyes of Wandil rain down geminids

where ancient Dod-men lie....)

II

By water now. Along the Lark to Bury
where by air the constellations
blaze down on these figures born of earth.

Was it before Beodricsworth became
Saint Edmund's town & shrine
that Sigebert's forebears paced off zodiacs

from Abbots Bridge to Stoke-by-Clare
discerned as fit propitiation still
by him who led the garlanded white bull

to its oblation for the barren girl
between imposing portals
of the Benedictine Abbey on the Lark?

By rivers then. Along this quiet one
past Bury where it forms
the tail of Sagittarius and on by sting

of Scorpio, by tribute and by tributary,
portaging on over Virgo
north of Shimpling to Chad Brook....

Where the Stour flows by Long Melford
they leaned into their journey, rowed along
the belly of the Lion close by Clare.

If Wandil gestured to the west, they
travelled east toward Harwich, backs against
the morning sun, oars against the tide.

Underbrush along the banks at first
held only otters, then at Mysteleigh solemn men
sat fishing, men knelt making salt;

at Manningtree, a single lighter hauled
the heavy stones up shallow higher reaches
where a mason waited with his tools

and visions of a chancel in his brain.
Stoke and Wilford built their low stone bridges then;
other towns built locks; local wool

brought bricks and lime and coal.
West to east, they met the horse-drawn barges,
passed young woodsmen felling trees

to build the *Thorn*, the *Syren* and the *Terpsichore*.
Lark by Stour by Orwell; Scorpio
by Lion. Moon by sun against the darkness.

Sun by moon. A giant with a sword....

III

Or with a ship. A *Syren* or a *Terpsichore*. And if a giant, then a giant metamorphosed over time. The man who'll six years later paint the *Hay Wain* may not know his river rises as a tiny brook east of the Chilterns in the Gogmagogs. And yet he feels the giant in it, yet he knows its gods. Today he finishes his sketch of Flatford Mill—the mill itself, the locks, the barge and bargemen, and the small distracted barefoot boy on his horse. He'll work it up in 1817 for the Academy and no one will complain that it lacks finish. The sketch itself is rough. He adds an ash—his favourite tree—some elms, a broken oak. He shades in clouds he's come to study with a meteorologist's precision. Then he shuts the sketch book and trudges off toward Dedham, marking in his mind the river's fringe of willowherb and reed, the rising heron and the darting snipe and redshank in the sky…

He wants to marry Charles Bicknell's daughter. He wants to paint this river and these shimmering green fields. He doesn't want to quarrel with Charles Bicknell, with the rector of his village, or with Bonaparte. And he doesn't want to paint for money portraits of the rich or of their homes: Malvern Hall, Petworth House, East Bergholt. The ships that followed *Thorn* on down the slips at Mistley shipyards belched a thousand years of Beltane fire at French sails on the Nile. Martello towers rose at Shotley and at Walton Ferry… But here and now it's quiet, he thinks. Here and now it's peaceful and the air is pure…

It's better to paint rivers than great houses.
It's better to be married than alone.
It's better with companionship to sit through winter nights
remembering the Stour in springtime
(or a cousin lying face-down in the mud at Waterloo).

Here, returned from London, nervous and annoyed,
bored by portraits that he's painted only months before
and talking to a friend who asks:
And what are you drawing landscapes for out here?

he picks a pinch of earth up off the path
they're walking and says *This!*

For this, he says.
This This This
For

    this

        *

This other ryver called of old time
Fromus maketh his beginning
near to Framlingham and then descendeth

close by Marlesford and so
southest of Farnham entertayneth yet
another ryver called the Gleme

which cometh out from Rendlesham
thus passing forth to Snapebridge and
contriving then his course to Yken

dedicates himself into the sea
not very far away from where the Stour & Orwell
run together into Harwich harbour.

Framlingham: Framela's people: strangers on
the Fromus before Fromus became Alde.
Folk who'd become burgen-holders paying 5d tax.

On the bluff above the mere the Bigods' castle
glowers: Henry's castle glowers back
from Orford. Herrings, cereals, pottery from

Staverton passed through the town, began a journey
inland or a journey to the coast.
Scratchings on the nave in Parham church

show navigable reaches: ships of little draft
came all the way from Normandy past
Orford, Slaughden, Iken, down this stream

that flows
into a pipe below a petrol station

      now

IV

      …Men will number
what they value most
in wills: "To Robert Cook my scalbote,

my anchor and the things belonging to it and
my spurling bote: to George Clare
my fysher, fartle, makerel nets & warropes:

To John Weylonde: A manfare of haryngnetts:
capstaynes, skewers & my sparling nets
that hangeth in the low to the sea this yere

and when the sparlyngfare is done the netts
schal then be partyd to my children:
Thomas, Christopher, Erasmus: ships belonging

to the havyn to be sold at Aldeburgh church."
The men who made the wills were fishermen;
The others built their boats along these shores…

or sold them victuals, or worked upon the land,
or herded sheep, kept inns, cut
the timber, prayed in church & monastery, wept

impressed at sea, took up piracy and smuggling,
made the malt that made the ale they drank,
organised themselves in unions, and were hanged.

By 1850 photographs appear to show us
what they looked like outside Newton Garrett's
maltings or beside their barges loading

at Snape quay. John Felgate, shipwright, has
no teeth and wears a cap of moleskins;
his son, standing by a dinghy, has a thick

mustache, a threadbare coat, & a determined gaze.
Jack Ward, skipper of the *Gladys*, smiles;
his heavy begrimed turtleneck presses up against

his graying whiskers and his wide square chin.
The carpenters, Alfred Andrews & his son,
look almost well-to-do beside the shipwrights;

the younger Andrews wears a tie, a waistcoat,
and a golden chain while sawing timber for a rudder
or a boom; Howell and Chatten, maltsters,

hold their massive wooden shovels, handles down,
and slop about in canvas boots. Their rugged faces
look like copper pennies in a winter sun.

If we could hear them speak we'd doubtless hear
them say how *chance-times a sloe-wind
brings old Tabbler Cable back to that same mawther*

who'd 'im clapper-clawed or hear them laugh about
the crones who *couldn't sculpt the roots
out as they got no teeth*. The carter thakketh his hors

upon the croupe and jumps up in his wagon.
He's off to town. The men who work the maltings
and the bargemen line up for their pay.

The bird that flies about them angling toward
the Orford Ness they call a *mavis;*
by the time it reaches sprawling spider-webs

of early-warning radar nets it's lost its name,
and anyone at Chantry Point
looking with binoculars for avocets or curlews

would only see, if it passed by, a thrush.
Along the ley-alignment point
at Sizewell, Beltane fires in the reactor

are contained by water drained out of the sea.

V

　　　　…But that the salt of say AD 500
should be drained from Deben marshes
that the land be sweet for corn and cattle…

That the river rising beyond Sutton, beyond
Woodbridge wait out flood & tide
for Norman engineers and then the Dutch,

for every local Fosdike, every local Waller
who might learn the warping
and the inning, reclaim with bank & seawall

or with sluice & gutter marshes then defended
by the reeves of Walton and
the men of Melton who might write: *lately salt,*

now fresh… That would take some time.
Some time, too, before the signals flash from
castle cresset, lucomb, lighthouse

or Martello tower up and down the coast
from Goseford to the Alde. No
early warnings here where everything's surprise.

South to north, they leaned into the journey,
rounded Landguard Point and
passed by Walton Castle, sailing with the tide

across the sand bar, steersman hugging
his athwartship tiller, small rain
in the oarsmen's eyes, wind across the stern.

Beyond the sandy heathland, the turf & bracken
over which they'd lug a ship the
size of this one to be buried as a cenotaph—

with coins from Usson-du-Poitou, a golden helmet,
maple lyre, & stone sceptre carved
with eight stern faces and a thin bronze stag

mounted on its delicate iron ring—
they reached the pools they sought and, anchoring
off mud flats, felled the trees,

built their timber halls beyond abandoned villas,
stayed at Hemley, Hatchley, Trimley,
called the river that they sailed "the deep one".

They'd say they lived in *Middanyeard,* where *haeleth
under heofenum:* they found themselves
between two seas… (the hero of their poem the sun).

Before them, Celts and Roman legions.
After them the Viking raids.
After them the Norman engineers and Flemish traders.

Before them, the single salters squatting
on the mud, the long walk for flints
along the Icknield Way. After them the excavation

of the buried ship…

*

Extensio. Eastern point
north of Southwold on the Easton Ness, now lost.
Portus Adurni. Was the Deben called Adurnus

by the Latins here and on the Alde?
Harbour, temperate climate, sheltered creeks—
and vines growing high above the cliffs.

Counts of the Saxon Shore constructed here
their fortress where they failed to hold the tide
against the kin of those first called

by Vortigern to fight his wars against the Picts.
(St Alban's first cartographer
would clearly mark his map: *Angulus Anglie*...)

Around the corner, then, and up the river
with the driftwood & the tide. Buoyed and beaconed,
spits and banks first marked with small

bouquets of yellow broom display their
angled emblems: Bowships beacon, Middleground,
Upper Waldringfield and Lower Ham,

Jack Rush beacon, Crimmy Moore, Horse Buoy.
If Edward were to anchor here
along the Kingsfleet, who but the Archbishop

might come sailing smartly out of Shotley
as the king, shining like some Helith, went to meet him
round into the Stour? On board the *Thomas*,

in a western wind, the Goseford ships impressed
for service, the power upon them
& Calais in fear, they'd break up the Great Seal.

So Wandil on the Stour gestures gravely
to the Wandil on the Gogmagogs. Against him lean
the sun & moon while all about him

widdershins there turns a circle of the dancers
who will help achieve the spring
as every ley south-east of Thetford Castle Mound

lines up along the tumuli and standing stones
to pass through places named for Bel
or Belus out to Walton on the northern Sea...

Beyond the Roman camp, the Saxon mound.
Beyond the Saxon mound the Viking
outpost in the Celtic forest with its secret paths.

Along the paths, the route to tributaries,
creeks, the sweetest hidden wells. Above the wells
a dowser with his twig, a Dod-man

with his sighting staves…

*

      who walks along the concrete wall,
and feels the fresh salt air,
and watches small yachts ply the quiet river

at high tide. Red sails, blue.
And bright white hulls. Woodbridge Sunday sailors
tack and jibe…

Alde by Stour by Deben. Ship by Saxon shore.
Cattle, corn by sea wall.
Dod-man, dowser, dapple of reflected cloud.

Wendy Mulford

At Thorpeness

"My Lover, The Sea": (The Tempest. Op. 109. Sibelius.)

I am waiting. This morning
it was Cap de Nez blue. Skimmering pale
barely blue, too light for early morning eyes.
We walked north, dog and I, up the sand strip towards the sea-kale nursery
Where the plants bloom, sporting
mementos like those who can sustain regard, knowing,
in their unruffled fruitfulness they are
worthy, undisturbed, on their shelved shingle bed.

& then
the phone rang to say you'd all be coming, now, soon, today,
imminently: don't get me wrong, of course I want you all
to be here—that's why I came after all—but now? Right now?
Oy veh!
In any relationship there are delicate moments,
early on when a thing might go forward, might stall, or
take off into a side-turning & never really dance again. That
Sea, is how I feel it is with us.
Through three days, from near-dawn until moon-up
I have studied your moods
your light your colour your
approach and your recoil.
I have followed beside you adapting myself
to your pace your remoteness &
your presence   picking up slips
of knowledge of your habits
from your daily traces learning to
recognise your voice your movements your smell
imprinting them on my flesh in my
heart
hearing them in my dreams

and when, like all lovers must be,
we are parted, I will cleave to you
& nothing and no one shall separate us.
Then a new lover with blue in her eyes
will walk beside you, open her heart and her ears to you
& discover you close to her pillow
troubling her sleep. You will slap at her feet
as you do in mischievous mood, or toss and growl
as you may, and you do, & she will try, vainly as I do,
to capture you on paper, in paint or stumbling words,
& find after all that you are snagged
beneath my jumper nearer
the heart than I had believed possible

& should I return
after absence I may find you
strangely changed
unfamiliar stripped
of your magic
as you might in the common light be seen
as only, entirely, essentially, nothing but
the sea:
an attribute or function of the larger concept, the seaside, the
picture postcard stuff, the place where families picnic people
shout & play beachball dogs splash ecstatic after
invisible lobbed pebbles,
a place out-of-season for the dedicated solitaries the
company of night-shore anglers to defy the cold and the winds in
windproof zip-up nylon, for small brave
night-lit boats to bob in pursuit of remnants of catches—
a sea like any other

The Question

About the shadow and the lip
        there may be
scar tissue
        never mind that
Somewhere
        the river runs down
where's home
the trees answer

    *

Such a poise can put the
        whole life in
question
        hesitancy holds
the clue

    *

Engage such a
        question
how do you know
        the size of the ocean?
Ask again
        then plunge

    *

If the moon rises
        above this cliff
does it rise too
        in your parlour?

    *

So. There is a clearing.
                    one tall pine bending
in the wind's commotion.
                  Soon the heart
will make its obligatory entry
                    sighing pining creating
more commotion

            *

There are more words here than are needed
         ...
And still their prison hulks disgrace us

           *

Take me down
            the winds
don't stop their howl

           *

It is not the place of time to tick
                what's worth five minutes
bliss?   a song, a tale
a joke of
            eternity

           *

So one leg's this side
                the estuary runs deep and cold
we may never reach the other

Claire Crowther

Warrener

Along the row of huts, *Lazy Jays, Icarus, Gull's Way, The Shoe*, and past the shabby row of smaller sheds without verandas, hearing you spell a wish-list of Christian names, *Elizabeth, Victoria, Queenie*, each halo of letters glowing over a red or white door like the orange damp around doorknobs and hinges, hearing the sea exhale

onto my feet, drag
shingle back in
again like oxygen,
Shalysim, Slepe.

Late autumn. Only one hut open. A woman, covered in fleece, eyes closed, in a deckchair listening to a sound,

lo sciabordio,
sea biting the shore.
I choose its wet
and gentle muzzle.

Choose to conceive. What is free will for?

Let's leave the boardwalk to catch the tiny crabs immured too long in casket manors of sand. Hearing lo sciabordio, they come out of the ebb, in a froth of low water.

R.F. Langley

The Ecstasy Inventories

We slow out and curve
then the deep lawlike
structures loom and bob
through. We sway up, shut
down and open, coolly, each
small hour. Quiet. Then
quieter still. When thin
rims of rose and powder-blue
start slightly and a marble
runs down a chute.

The beach is stocked with one cobble
and another until you have to be
particular. Which are these tiny kickshaws
or tricky grenades on the old mud peppered
for ten thousand years. I've been noticing
how they needed low light and stale eyes
to catch such humble cajolery, all along,
hatching with soft pops into articulate
habits or costumes or clothes in a great
press: the broad, the heavy, the paragon,
her most scarlet gowns.

A blackamoor spurs by. The picture
of an Moore on horseback. Who
next? In a wink, in a pinked
petticoat, in a waistcoat set
with spots like pinks, in one
worked with eyes, she ambles
the lanes. An Moore on
horseback. The picture
of an Moore on horseback.
St Jerome. Mr Coke's mother.
Worked with eyes. Blue eyes.

The warm sun in some June. This June.
Both Junes. Take now and make a then.
A room. A roomy workshop. Elderflowers.
Forget the scent. Here is a carpenter,
singing. It is a hymn. Never mind
the scent, forget the difficult
bushes. Here is the hymn
from this contented man,
who cuts a shield upon a mantelpiece,
good humoured and intelligent, but the
cool, slow-motion, vanilla, bombs, ribboning…

The cuffs, collar and bedclothes
have lace on them. The lace can be
mentioned as strips with discs
or wheels, as sunbursts
of logical straps, rays, pips,
split pods or crooked stars, as
much as counting and nice
as a pocketbook with every
species, in flight, at rest,
in colour. These inroads let
me understand, and mark
sharply. Over what? Over
brilliant quietness. The path
ends in the shadow of trees.
In the trees I can't see the tiny
passerines all about in the
sparkling confusion. Or
her cheeks. Or her chin.

Follow the come on to the regular
heart, where we shall read a long
page. O my friend! The thrilled
ripples and cicalas and the dark
where the path and the story
beat through! Boreas did love her,
here, illustriously, with cicalas
and rippling. I can hear some
Hippocentaur's lips take hold

of grass with the resilience of
grass and that old ripping sound.

Silver moon; thatch; owl on the gable
and twelve silver instruments on the desk
for surgery. Silver moon on the desk.
Twelve silver instruments constellate
behind clouds. Ready for the straw
bird in the house of feathers. Mild
fingers set twelve silver straws on
the shining wood. There is a soft
interjection, stroboscopic starlight
and the powers realign. In another
box there are two gold rings.

No virtuoso in the glade. Just
heaviness in the darkened boughs
and twigs akimbo say I must
leave my father, try to go, months
ago. Dancing Mickey tossed
his chin and both his arms so
that the yellow gloves shot
glittering out and curved
sadly away. Gone, in a rigmarole
of little evil grass. Come
to pass.

White hedonism cut on blue
intelligence and laced
with silver anxiety. Bravo.
It braces milady's cortical
layer to take what could
have been trauma but now snugs
a bee in a comfort. While ants
silkily fidget and moderate
men press on, juddering,
grinning, being temperate
because of the price of beer.

Fold pack away; there is no crash.
Amongst the carnivorous thus and
thus and thus come two grey eyes
as you think, "Is it a comma's wings
make such a silky noise?" So the
grogram, the paragon, snarl. So
fighting for their ranges the
wolves forget the deer. Or they
would hunt them out. Peace.
Famine. In the border zones
the butterflies are all eyes.

In heaven, where they don't
refurnish often, there will
still be an old white bodice
cut on blue and two lost
roses. Sure, in Walpolelane
there is a whirlwind of old
clothes. You would have thought.
Until a closer look saw each
was not vexed but folded
in unexpected readiness
in the press of the storm.

Andrew Brewerton

The Stoveplate

for Roger Langley

Her starling eye a long way fallen
In the chimney searches through a fluke
Of slant daylight, a lost lens winking

Late-on in the opened stoveplate
Of an August afternoon. Bird-curious is
The inclination of her neck & yellow

The little moon in her beak: a nice gloss
In the nave at Cratfield. Our two Ruths
Then Eric, look in turn. The stove lid opens

Closes. Soon we'll make this further eye
Of daylight in the south door, & looking out
Askance from eye to eye she'll skip until

The startled space will shiver with departing.
What can we say, that is not given? To whom
Address the staved attention of this air?

Why I lifted the cold stoveplate won't recount.
The moon's unnumbered sequence circles
Still. The bird enclosure sequels don't amount.

Our children shout delight in what they will.

Rodney Pybus

Spitting Distance

It takes hours to trudge to the end
of this spit of shifting particular grains
and sea-smoothed cobbles:

you walk gingerly as if the flint bird's
eggs were not solid, or you were trying
to go across time without being seen,

all the minutes twisting
under your soles. Here you're exposed
as anywhere, on this Anglian beach,

feeling an idiot on the flat earth,
cloud, grass, dune, turnstone keeping low
under the enormously shifting sky.

The gale's straight down from the pole
or driving west from the steppes:
it's so lazy (she used to say)

it just goes straight through you,
so that you feel you're beginning
to chill from the centre outwards.

It behaves like a screw-loose colourist
dashing its black rage over wet paper.
Shapes, you observe, even here, but on the run.

Nearly at the end, you see the only
remaining strand is breaking up,
a handful at a time going down

into the widening channel, the tide picking up
force and speed. All you have left is the need.
The gulls pick up the flattened cries

of *Weep!* and throw them away, again
and again. The wind does not give up,
nor the birds, nor the battering minutes.

Silly Season

On its season seely Suffolk swings giddy
and in the first week of February,
sky grey as a slaty-back

but mild as maybe, I listen
without belief, cannot trust my
sight of that fluting, fluttery

speck—is it spring, or the millennium or
the overheating of downtrodden, resilient Terra?
It surely is (and the only sure things

in this life are miracles, but why?)
a lark, unreeling, untangling the threads
of his song, ancient in its freshness, high

climbing almost out of sight,
climbing till he may be something on the eye,
but the notes still falling brightness

from just imaginable tiers of heaven
no less divine because merely sky,
and seely Suffolk swings giddy on its season.

Speaking of Angels

I don't believe in angels
(even when I can see them lined up more than fifty feet

above my head
back to back in pairs as if uncertain about what's to be or not)

I'm quite impervious
to the pale curtains they wear for dresses, their gold-plate

haloes and curls
and bed-time story wings like quattrocento Disney

supposed to make you
trust the status of their prequels and special announcements

The ones above me now
I can see by the clerestory's falling light were once spangled

in red and green and silver—
so high up they escaped Cromwell's lads on the rampage in 1644

and I will admit to
their faded wooden charms… but the kind of inspired uttering

I can take more happily
on trust comes from the crafty player of a baryton

that's like a rare enhanced viol
a cello look-alike with secret strings whose plucked notes as well as bowed

tell me something
more persuasive, not to say heavenly, from their steel and gut—

that what's most sublime
is what's most human, soaring right up to the startled angels

and beyond,
their wings outstretched like transfixed fliers

(say, silver-streaked
hawk moths or some other casual migrants)

as if unable
to resist this awkward truth but still gaping in disbelief

Charlotte Geater

broken fingers

i am strapped in
        & saw open-top buses
        ghosting through ipswich
we by derelict /
        we—saw the burnt-out factory, drank in the fog
          ready ——————
                          for ——————
                                        what?

it rained all summer.
        & sometimes it is just rain.

it is history here. the same men
sunburnt flap the sails under
skies like fat crackle/&
        brine but we have a labour

        party that won't support
    strikes & a protest movement that
is no #clusterfuck i mean
they massage each other in unison.

yr hair is so clean.

there is only smoke & seawater, no, mouths the river
spits the docks fills the seats—
        cracked plastic lets it all in.

tapped our fingers together
pink woozy
        nails—my eyes wide the size

of yr freckles. the sky

of a shop window blinks & we pierced
our ears, noses, nipples,
teeth.

ready to become burnt sugar again.

      i waited for the thunder, ready
for there to be no such town again.
i mean a suburb / a service station
at least somebody would have a job.
we'd be so lucky. & the left,

what have we left? when you've washed
& you're able to say

syndicalist, no, i am a fuchsia-eyed
sharp little knife & i have thought about everything.
i mean it. i mean

      i remember when all of this

    was dead blue,
    a month full of seawater.
    a mouth full of rain.

a sponge pulses & scalds its heart.
will not work. are you clean yet.
try saline.

if you don't want to be sick
then yr not doing it right.

Zoë Skoulding

Orion

stars stream information out of date
before it gets here sky fills half
the field of vision he replays his son's
steps or his own or chewing gum
stuck in the pocket of secondhand jeans
in 1978 an embroidery knotting the past
in place or fraying ways through
what time cuts up as the story cuts
across the short edge of the field drawing
forgotten paths into itself the lines
of memory static in blood and baying

I balance the world in my ears a mess
of crushed feathers a smell of damp
behind the door creaking open over
stone the scent of infrastructures
east to west now an owl circles
soil shifts from clay to sand
the rattle of his father's lungs
as something's torn apart in dark
meat on my tongue we grow fat
on history bright bodies in playback
move before you can see them

Orford

The castle safe in its demesne
(an oyster cradling seed
pearls around a f(r)iction)
is ringed with small hills,
looks out, not in.

The wild man of the sea
(tortured because he wouldn't speak)
outswam his captors:
sun flames on the blue reach,
the sea tilting up like a knife.

Fish leap, the water shines
on undrowned voices while we
(Sizewell soft in its
shell on the horizon)
swallow oysters and pepper,
the whole story.

Deryn Rees-Jones

Midnight Beach at Sizewell B

How ordinary it is,
like a shoebox, or a series of shoeboxes,
as if you could assemble it yourself,
make the dome complete, for instance, in a trice,
splitting two straight lines in half
then bending them
till they become two softly touching arcs,
made pale and oddly solid,
silvered in a moment,
a gasp of breath on glass.
Yet still it would be nothing more than ordinary—
in fact it's this you can accept it for—
the line of cars, the lights, its gently low-key whirr,
the men and women on their shift
now laughing, muttering, perhaps, while
diligently clocking on; one tiny, smoking chimney
straying in the starless sky
as if all human error, pain
was quietly taken care of, here—
bundled up, smoothed out, and trimmed;
catapulted centuries away.

Aidan Semmens

Hauling a Boat (Sutton Hoo)

Tugged by the tide one way & the wind
the other, tan sails tightly furled,
the barge turns & turns about
at anchor in midstream

whimbrel at the water's edge
white underfeathers ruffled
by the breeze a gull
steps sideways on the surfline

sweat breaks out on a muggy day
soft fruit crushed under the hull
staining straining legs & hands
a bloody purple

for a royal interment
on the hill fires rise
the wind keeps watch
we sow a perfect turf

for lawns & bowling greens
below the ritual burial-ground
of the navigator king
a wool-master's alabaster

encased within a nave
of finely jointed timbers
carving the billows
of a cloud-scudded sky

shrouds rattle in the harbour
& metal masts whistle

while white breakers tumble
among the sun & shadows

swallows swoop & swerve
readying for departure
the rails' precise curve
simplifies the line of the river

Return to the Pleasure Beach

all night the harvester's out
bright lights & machinery
for lifting of the beet

an age-old tradition
vanished into shadowplay
unhurried tranquillity
turbulence & unrest
the earliest
            known setting
of the mass for the dead

what can I do
with a single note? sparse
yearning lines
            a piano
grows in a year from timber planks
to its own unique voice

an illicit affair in a small town
grainy & unfinished
polyphonic twists
stark power
raw beauty
a lookout tower
over the uncertain shore

explorations
of sound in space

a ruined boat
half buried in the fen
pitched headlong into intoxicating
colours
   lunar
shimmerings
     pungent ideas
blowing the dust off
forward propulsion

shifting coastline
Martello towers
& a stump
of old tree, roots
fatally steeped in brine

the harpsichord
      breaks
the shackles of convention
genial warmth with echoes
of klezmer & jazz
lustrous viola

sweet stinky cargo
hauled on the reach
redundancies of toilage in the silt
sluice seepages meander deeply etched
to the edge of the mud

a walk among saints
in moated grounds, a tenacious
coastal village
    fishing
& smuggling succeeded
50 years ago
    by the Magnox reactor

drawing in seawater as
an abundant coolant
                         a meditation
on light, energy, the collapse of time
our ambitious
                methods of survival

the Spitfire pilot is also its rescuer
salvaged engine crafted new
by each carefully engineered
turn of the lathe, screw
& turbine, Merlin torque & marque

maquette precision, oiled
to an exact approximation of wear
smell, note & rhythm redolent
of a youth before ours

new footage of the first performance
gesture & structure shaped
with meticulous
fingerwork at Harvard
gothic architecture of the cathedral
nave, sea-going
barque on inland waters

conjuring the last judgement
with the ghost of Bartók
complex minimalism
rhythmic mouse-clicks amplified
to dance & burlesque

precise routes plotted
between
                eastern Europe
& the cafés of Buenos Aires
half the world's population
of grey seals is found
around British coasts

waders at the water's margin
turnstone redshank curlew dunlin
colours mutable with the day's changing mood
somewhere a gull or crow
surprised from its meal
godwit squadrons slice the cooling air

humidity is a key requirement
holes may be chiselled
to a depth of four inches
(the cimbalom anchors
pungent bagatelles
to the heritage of Benny Goodman)
both sexes can drum
trunks & branches
continuing
           until late June

adults feed mainly on cuckooflower
betony, fleabane & buttercup
in complicated sleep
a rusting wing
among scorched nettles

the turnip pile's gone
these ten years

Michael Laskey

The Corpse

He shares my morning cup of tea, likes it
colder than me. Staring at the empty
blue window, he's my dad propped up
glimpsed again through the ward's swing doors.
I reach for my book, find my place
or jump up quick, wash, give myself
a close shave, inhale soap, and froth
the strong teeth he bares at the mirror.
He's a rude child. I rattle him off
downstairs, stop his mouth with muesli,
fresh fruit. Once I'd kiss him at the school
gates and get on with my life.
But he grows so fast. No time since
he was nothing but a blink in my eye,
a blank at the end of my tunnel,
yet self-evident now, so conspicuous
in the tube some woman stands up
and offers me her seat. Though my feet
are killing me, I decline, my smile
tightened by his grin. He knows me
inside out. He's like a parent
come to collect me from a party
I've just started to enjoy. Ridiculously
punctual. Oh, he can wait. Yes, he can wait.
And he does, exchanging ghastly
benign glances with that corpse
of yours at the way we fret
over deadlines or how badly we've slept.

Close

Over these last few days
of black ice, iron frost,
of Tim going in and out
packing, hardly speaking,
I keep on finding myself
in that check-out queue again
behind them, my eyes resting
on the child on his mother's hip,
sucking his thumb, half-asleep,
while the fingers of his other hand
twitch and nibble at her neck.
The woman, head turned away,
paying attention to her friend,
seems not to notice any more
than the glazed-eyed baby,
except that she hitches him up
and is holding him now, I'd guess,
just a little more closely.

Herbert Lomas

Sea Lady

Someone's crept out of the sea,
lying on the pebbles, in pain:
like a crippled labrador.
She raises one arm, a lady
in a siesta, languidly,
though night's falling, and this January rain.

Hearing my crunch on the shingle,
she's turning bitch-soft eyes and whiskers to vet me.
I'm coming too close,
and she growls, hisses and whispers,
tensing my tail with her speech,
though I know she can't get me.

Hurt? Perhaps she's tired?
But I'm too close, so she levers her spine
and flops down on a shingle bank, enters the ocean,
periscopes twice with her head,
then hoists ashore,
crutching her legless rear up the steep incline.

Who'd be sick, if they lived in the ocean?
And who'd bark
so hard after fish, they'd give up the earth,
lose hands and legs,
freezing the warm blood back
to the cold, to feel after fish in the dark?

I sit in my lights by the fire, listening to Mozart,
reading Gibbon.
A Diocletian legionary, an old lag
looking for loot, found

a beautiful leather purse of priceless pearls.
He threw the swag away and kept the bag.

For what's no use can have no value.
And in the morning she
who loves the water I left behind
is gone like a piece of flotsam,
a bag of pearls,
that is and always will be far out at sea.

The Wild Swans at Aldeburgh

Some days they look like outsize geese
with no secret, seen
waddling across reclaimed land
to a ditch. Thirteen:
my lucky number. But one, hatched out too late,
is without a mate.

The trees are in their winter grandeur.
A line of pine trees stands
aware of me as I of them—
children holding hands.
We watch a ditch ruffle like elephant skin
and the sun whiten and thin.

I track a curlew in a cloud
by its call: fast headway.
The thirteenth swan has taken off:
an immature grey,
it creaks a low flight, then stands and walks alone,
feeling its half-soul gone.

Pathetic these fallacies our lives fatten.
Forty years are lost
since I first read Yeats, yet I never see
a swan without his ghost.

A swan in death and I in life both read
the bobbin, rewinding the thread.

December sunshine brings white joy,
a milky hole in light.
These weeks three friends or almost-friends
have taken that silver flight
to some new pond or ditch or reclaimed land.
As souls, or swans, we stand
in a place of no giving in marriage.
Aware or unaware,
a leap through inarticulate light
defines some strangled prayer,
leaving us stripped, deciduous winter trees,
hand in hand, or on our knees.

Night Fishing

They sit on the shoreline, under
a green umbrella, wielding quidsworth
of equipment and catching a few whiting.

At the eye clinic, behind me, a lady said,
She's so much older than him, you know.
She won't leave him alone. He's had to

take up night fishing. But no: they munch
a sandwich under the wind, share it
with their dog and stare at the silver

the moon's unrolling to their feet,
feeling how the world was before it was
so well-organised and understood,

and in the dawn a red ball rises
swiftly out of the sea
and disappears inside a cloud like a god.

Anne Beresford

The Chariot

We were walking across the heath,
the sun bright on purple and yellow,
his cloak brushed the heather
as he spoke of things to come
and of what was past.
There was no reason to leave him.
"Today will be the day," he said.

And then in the distance a cloud
shimmering on the horizon.
The larks fell silent
as a stranger music shook the ground,
and the cloud coming nearer
shaped as a chariot drawn by winged horses.
Their fire swept between us
parting us for ever.

At that moment when my bowels cringed with fear—
no, awe—the sign I'd prayed for,
without knowing why, was upon me,
searing through my fragile shadow,
this nameless identity,
organs, germs, microbes, atoms,
part of a universe still full of mystery.
There was no companion, had never been.
I was alone between sea and heather,
holding a cloak of darkness in hands
which seemed suddenly alien.

Suffolk Future

Once, those were trees
and this stinking tarmac
rolled long shadowed
in late sun
towards the sea.

Collar-doves
mournful all summer.

The worlds we inhabited
were separate
yet connected.

The house stood there—
just there
where cars and lorries thunder by—
the gate opened with a click
your skirt brushing against
willow herb
as you rang the bell.
You rang the bell, because
you said, it woke
the silence.

We walked along the cliffs
lit by brilliant gorse
and once, were lost for hours
in heather
looking for the path
to lead us home.

The sea splashes forlorn
on an empty beach
listening to the buzz of power.

This car park
is a garden of remembrance

where we sat on a worn bench
and counted butterflies
resting on the sunny wall.
The leaves, flowers, long grass
almost enveloped us.

Were we warned
did we warn anyone?
And the new world
miles and miles of concrete desolation
and talk of progress.

I search for you
my love,
in the deep of my head
not lost but gone before
as it were.

Will Stone

Reeds in November

In November they reach
homeward rooks without touching them
and the water spreads to the muddy edge,
paint on silk, blood in a shoe.
The reeds choir escaping air,
the seen nutrient their brittle gills
loose over walkers, sculptures, watchers.
They lean in a wave then rise
supporting the body that bypasses us
and dies out as arranged
in the space between
competing gulls.

Greyfriars

Late afternoon is the time for that path,
when the light fails and the iron gates of Greyfriars
eerily brand the shadow with cowled monks.
It's best when the light fails down that path
skirting the meagre cliff top copse,
where in February a brook of snowdrops
bubbles up, and the balm of sea sound
rolls back beneath the bridge with its baby arch.
Inexpressible melancholy drew them,
Thomas, Fitzgerald, Swinburne,
their footfalls weighed, compressed, absorbed
by thick fir foliage and the slow scrape of birdsong.
Rhododendrons, dark peat paths and sounds
flickering on dead leaves—frail skeletal feet
or the first drop feelers of a downpour?
You proceed due east to the light.
Suddenly the land has had enough,
shrubs long extinct fling themselves out,
strung with cries and madly racing cloud.
You face once more that scythe of slate
lipped by jaundiced surf, the gore of cliffs,
the sluiced shore where horses plod,
heaving the dark barrows of their blood
northwards then south.

Richard Caddel

Shiner

Walk in a favourite place under
stars and around knapped flint.
You walking never still grew there,
it was a dark and stormy

Christmas. Long ago. Wind out of
northeast, waders grounded, memory.
Children singing as if forever
and everything green and

wet, moving to a new time by what
means it can. Your mum and I
whisper how much we miss
going together to meet it.

Michael Hamburger

In the Country

1

In May and June, this Election year,
Slugs grew fat as never before
And the little snails, too, took their shares,
Stripping the lupin heads bare,
Quenching the red-hot poker,
Reduced to a slimy stump as it made to rise.

Grey daylight lingered, the summer solstice
Came and passed by.
Nettles grew tall as never before
And cleaver, bindweed proliferated
To strangle what they had not smothered,
Bloated slugs could not swallow
Or cuckoospit cover.

2

As village idiot talk
Sensible people laughed off
Subversive mutters about a Flood:
The Drizzle, you mean, the Long Drizzle,
Is what they said;
But not when they slithered or slipped
On floor tiles that sweated.

3

Nor when the non-Flood's bedraggled Noah
Trying each day to keep seed alive on this Earth
For another term, for a season that sunshine would bless,
But soaked to the skin for his pains till dry clothes ran out,
With catarrh and sciatica, pleurisy and pneumonia
Took to his bed in the end.
Empty, his ark drifted off.
Into delirium even no dove bore one sprig or leaf,

4

Though farther afield work was in progress,
Progress at work. They were widening the lanes
For access to the construction site
Of another nuclear power station
Approved for the Heritage Coast,
Next to the Bird Reserve, the protected marshes
Of dwindling wild orchid and meadowsweet.
Costly, of course, retractable eyes could gather
From computer printouts, columns and columns of figures,
The calculations they trust
More than they trust their own senses, their hearts and heads
Or the soul that on Sundays they still may profess to be theirs;
But, in this age of the mollusc, a source
Of profit once more to the greedy feeders;
And, for the moment, no greater danger to them
Than the various poisons on land, in water and air
They believe they are thriving on, in their coats of mucus
Or movable shelters, their shells.

5

All July and August, with breaks as reminders of summer,
Skies remained veiled, the ground sodden.
Neither cherry nor plum could ripen,
But split, then rotted, unpicked.
Great hailstones battered holiday-makers,
Shattered greenhouse roofs.
Near house walls, yield of the nights,
Lay corpses of long-eared bats.

6

The non-Flood's Noah recovered, planning another ark,
Proof against radiation and acid rain,
Air-conditioned, capacious enough to provide for
One breeding pair of every species known to be extant
At the blueprint stage—and, this time, of plants as well.
The question was, who could build it, when such technology
Was reserved for profit-making and war,
When the funds must be raised by private subscription
And that vessel was almost a second Earth.

Winter Evenings, East Suffolk

The sun's and our days are shortening
While before solstice the visible moon fills out,
What on these lowland wide horizons lingers
As though to reiterate recall, is dusk:
On the south-western from flame to glimmer
Slowly the glow subsides
From scarlet to roseate, amber drifts and shifts
Or else to a strip of blue
Deeper than any a summer noon sustained.
If a black cloud hangs there it shines
Rimmed with departing light.

December's last leafage responds:
A red so dark on this maple
It's nightfall too, detained,
Wisps of pale yellow to ochre
On the rugosa stems wilting
As on those with buds for another year.

Then, moon not yet full, whole skies
Whether clouded or clear
Are silver tarnishing.

Never a night is total
Until our vision, dimmed,
Disowns the shapes, the shadows,
All colours mixed on palettes too far away.

Notes on the Poets

Part 1

Algernon Charles Swinburne
A.C. Swinburne (1837-1909) had the misfortune, when not yet quite 30, to be hailed as Tennyson's successor as the greatest living British poet, a dubious distinction he retained in orthodox public opinion until his death. It did not prevent him from producing enormous quantities of verse, plays, several novels, works on Shakespeare, Jonson and Blake, and contributions to the *Encyclopaedia Britannica*, or from being nominated six times in seven years for the Nobel Prize in Literature. Born in London, brought up on the Isle of Wight, educated at Eton and Oxford, he travelled widely and wrote nature poetry based on a variety of mostly British landscapes: 'By the North Sea' (1880), set on the eroding cliffs and beach at Dunwich, is widely considered to be among his best work.

Henry Howard, Earl of Surrey
Surrey (1517-47), first cousin of Anne Boleyn and himself of royal descent on both sides, was from age 12 brought up at Windsor with Henry VIII's illegitimate son Henry Fitzroy. He grew up to become a soldier, an occasional brawler, and a writer of satires, lyrics and sonnets; two of his better-known poems, 'Prisoned in Windsor', and 'Satire Against the Citizens of London', describe occasions when he was imprisoned on fair or false charges. "The Poet Earl" fatally fell foul of the long antagonism between the Howard and Seymour families when he was indicted for treason in January 1547, and executed on Tower Hill. His father and son, both Thomas Howard, were both dukes of Norfolk, their seat being Framlingham Castle; his own tomb is not the grandest of the Howard monuments in St Michael's church in Framlingham, but it is the most colourful.

Ann Candler
"*ANN CANDLER*, the author of the following poems, is in the plainest and humblest sense of a word, a Cottager: she has never had a higher station, or, in this world, a higher aim; but, if virtuous principles, pure and modest manners, a deep sense of religion, and steady unaffected Christian faith, are the best guides to a happy immortality, she will not be the least or lowest in the mansions of the blessed." So begins the introduction to the volume of her *Poetical Attempts* that was published, with a long subscription list, in 1803. Candler, born in Yoxford in 1740, was the self-educated daughter of a glover. Twice abandoned, the first time for six years, the second permanently, by her hard-drinking soldier husband, by whom she had a total of eight children, she spent many years in the workhouse and would undoubtedly have ended her days there but for the support of the now anonymous clergyman who arranged for her poems—many of which first appeared in the *Ipswich Journal*—to be collected and published.

Her best poems deal with details of her own hard life, her less successful ones with the public affairs of the day. She died at Holton in 1814 at the age of 74, having lived the last 12 years of her life at Copdock, under a roof of her own.

ANNA LAETITIA BARBAULD

Anna Laetitia Barbauld, née Aikin (1743-1825) had a successful writing career at a time when female professional writers were rare, and is considered one of the founders of English Romanticism. Educated at home in Leicestershire by her mother, she married Rochemont Barbauld, a minister, in 1772 and with him set up and ran the Palgrave Academy, a Dissenters' school in north Suffolk. Surprised by the success of her *Poems,* which appeared in 1772 and ran to four editions, she went on to write *Lessons for Children* (1779) and *Hymns in Prose for Children* (1781), which remained in print for over a century and are credited with revolutionising the teaching of reading. After leaving Suffolk for Hampstead in 1783 she went on to write political essays, calling for the abolition of slavery, equal rights for non-Anglicans, and an end to war. Her verse satire *Eighteen Hundred and Eleven* (1812), which blamed British participation in the Napoleonic wars for what she saw as the decline of the nation and empire, was so badly received she gave up writing and retired from public life.

GEORGE CRABBE

"Tho' nature's sternest painter, yet her best"—this assessment by Byron is quoted on the memorial to George Crabbe (1754-1832) in St James's church, Trowbridge, Wiltshire, where for the last 17 years of his life Crabbe was rector. It is with his birthplace at Aldeburgh that Crabbe is mostly associated, however, though in the course of his life he had a remarkable number of Suffolk addresses—schools in Bungay and Stowmarket, a doctor's practice and farm in Wickhambrook, then Woodbridge, where he met his wife and wrote his first published poems; later Parham, Great Glemham and Rendham. After being taken up by Edmund Burke he moved for a time in exalted artistic circles in London without ever losing touch with his humble roots, his compassion for the common man or his scientific fascination with the natural world. A friend of Wordsworth, Coleridge and Southey, Crabbe developed a narrative writing style that effectively formed a bridge between the Augustan poetry epitomised by Alexander Pope and a Wordsworthian Romanticism. His collection *The Borough* (1810)—i.e. Aldeburgh—is effectively a set of short stories in verse; Benjamin Britten took from it the tale of 'Peter Grimes' for his opera of that name.

ROBERT BLOOMFIELD

Crabbe's younger contemporary Robert Bloomfield (1766-1823) is in many ways a similar writer, though his aim was more straightforwardly documentary of rural life. Born in Honington, where his widowed mother ran the village school, he worked in his teens as a farm labourer, gaining the experience which would put the stamp of authenticity on the extraordinary detail in his long poem 'The Farmer's Boy' (1800). Written while he was working as a cobbler in London, the poem made his name, selling 25,000 copies in two years, going into several editions in America and being translated into French, German, Italian— and Latin. Its admirers included Southey and John Constable, two of whose paintings are of scenes from the poem. Despite this success, and the ensuing *Rural Tales, Ballads and Songs* (1802), Bloomfield died, as he was born and had mostly lived, in poverty.

Bernard Barton

Though born in Carlisle, Bernard Barton (1784–1849), known as 'The Quaker Poet', went to school in Ipswich and lived most of his life in Woodbridge, where he worked as a bank clerk. The father-in-law of Edward FitzGerald, well-known translator of the *Rubáiyát of Omar Khayyám,* Barton was well respected as a writer in his time, though his verse has not aged well. His chief works are *The Convict's Appeal* (1818), a protest against the death penalty, and *Household Verses* (1845); he also wrote a large number of hymns.

Part II

Andy Brown

Director of the Centre for Creative Writing at Exeter University, Andy Brown studied ecology, an interest and way of thinking that informs much of his poetry. He was previously centre director for the Arvon Foundation's creative writing courses, and has been a recording musician. His most recent book of poems is *The Fool and the Physician* (London: Salt Publishing, 2012). His poems here come from *Fall of the Rebel Angels: Poems 1996-2006* (Salt, 2006) and *Goose Music* (Salt, 2008).

Angela Leighton

Professor Angela Leighton, senior research fellow at Trinity College, Cambridge has published books on Shelley, Elizabeth Barrett Browning, Victorian women poets and, most recently, *On Form: Poetry, Aestheticism, and the Legacy of a Word* (Oxford: OUP, 2008). Her poetry titles are *A Cold Spell* (Nottingham: Shoestring Press 2000), *Sea Level* (Shoestring, 2007) and *The Messages* (Shoestring, 2012).

Tamar Yoseloff

Tamar Yoseloff was born in the USA in 1965. Since moving to London in 1987, she has been reviews editor of *Poetry London* magazine, and from 2000 to 2007, programme coordinator for The Poetry School; she now works as a freelance creative writing tutor. Her first full collection of poetry, *Sweetheart* (Nottingham: Slow Dancer Press 1998), won that year's Aldeburgh Festival Prize; her most recent is *Formerly* (London: Hercules Editions, 2012), a collaboration with photographer Vici MacDonald. She has a house in Suffolk and is a frequent visitor to the county.

Ronald Blythe

Ronald Bythe, the doyen of writers in and about Suffolk, is probably best known for his oral histories, especially *Akenfield: Portrait of an English Village* (London: Allen Lane; New York: Pantheon, 1969), which won the Heinemann Award in 1969 and was the basis for Peter Hall's 1974 film *Akenfield*. His reputation as a keen-eyed (and keen-eared) observer of rural life can only have been enhanced by his latest memoir, *At the Yeoman's House* (London: Enitharmon Press, 2011). Though less noted as a poet than as a writer of prose, he has always been a lover and champion of poetry and it seems characteristic that his Desert Island Discs selection, when he was a guest of the Radio 4 series in 2001, should have been a recording of Ted Hughes reading John Clare's poem 'The Nightingale's Nest'.

Victor Tapner

Victor Tapner's extraordinary sequence *Flatlands* (London: Salt Publishing, 2010), winner of the East Anglian Book Award, dramatises the lives and concerns of prehistoric dwellers throughout the region now known as East Anglia. Though few of the poems have a specifically identifiable location, 'Iceni' references the tribe who gave their name to the Suffolk village of Iken. A former *Financial Times* journalist, Tapner has also written a political thriller, *Cold Rain* (London: Grafton, 1988).

Pauline Stainer

Pauline Stainer's *The Lady and the Hare: New and Selected Poems* (Tarset: Bloodaxe Books, 2003) draws on eight previous collections. She has since published *Crossing the Snowline* (Bloodaxe, 2008) and *Tiger Facing the Mist* (Bloodaxe, 2013). Her work is deeply imbued with a sense of place, history and myth, as exemplified here in 'Little Egypt', which brings together elements drawn from Orkney, where she lived for some years, and the Saxon burial site at Sutton Hoo. She now lives in Hadleigh, Suffolk.

John Matthias

Born in Ohio in 1941, John Matthias, who for many years taught at the University of Notre Dame in Indiana and continues to co-edit the *Notre Dame Review*, has been described by the American writer Guy Davenport as "one of the leading poets of the USA". During the 1970s and '80s he was visiting fellow in poetry at Clare Hall, Cambridge, and for part of that time lived at Hacheston in Suffolk, where his wife hails from. His many books of poetry include the Shearsman collections *Trigons* (2010), *Collected Longer Poems* (2012) and *Collected Shorter Poems* in two volumes (2011 and 2013); Shearsman also published a book of memoirs and essays, *Who Was Cousin Alice? & Other Questions* (2011), at the same time as Salt Publishing produced *The Salt Companion to John Matthias*, edited by Joe Francis Doerr.

WENDY MULFORD
Welsh-born Wendy Mulford has in the past been associated with Cambridge, Marxism, feminism, and the "British Poetry Revival" of the 1970s. As founder of Street Editions, and later co-editor with Ken Edwards of the amalgamated Reality Street Editions, she has published many of the most notable poets of the British avant-garde. Books she has written or edited include *This Narrow Place* (London: Pandora 1988), a biography of the writers Sylvia Townsend Warner and Valentine Ackland, *Virtuous Magic: Women Saints and Their Meanings* (with Sara Maitland. London: Continuum, 1997) and *The Virago Book of Love Poetry* (1990 & 1998). Her poetry has been widely anthologised; her 13 collections include two co-written with Denise Riley, and *The East Anglia Sequence: Norfolk 1984—Suffolk 1994*. She has lived in Suffolk since the mid-1990s and in 2008 produced a joint collection, *Whistling Through the Nightwood* (Colchester: Orphean Press), with three other poets featured here: Anne Beresford, Herbert Lomas and Pauline Stainer.

CLAIRE CROWTHER
Widely published in magazines and anthologies, Claire Crowther has worked as a consumer journalist, an editor and communications director and was poet-in-residence in 2008 at the Dorich House museum in Kingston-on-Thames. Her book *Stretch of Closures* (Exeter: Shearsman Books, 2007), from which the poem 'Warrener' is taken, was shortlisted for the Aldeburgh Best First Collection prize. All the beach huts named in the poem can be seen on the seafront at Southwold.

R.F. Langley (1938-2011)
The grand memorial in the chancel of St Andrew's church, Bramfield, by Nicholas Stone to Arthur Coke, who died in 1629, and his wife Elizabeth, is possibly the finest piece of seventeenth-century sculpture in Suffolk; it was what first brought Roger and Barbara Langley to the county in the 1960s, leading to many holidays and eventually to them moving to the village in 1999 on his retirement from a career as a grammar-school teacher in the West Midlands. Langley's drawing of Elizabeth Coke's carved lace, described, along with an inventory of their possessions, in 'The Ecstasy Inventories', provided both the title and the front cover of his first collection, *Hem* (Cambridge: Infernal Methods, 1978). Although Langley lived for most of his life in south Staffordshire, the inspiration for much of his work came from the landscapes of Suffolk. His ten published books include *Collected Poems* (Manchester: Carcanet Press, 2000), *Journals* (Exeter: Shearsman Books, 2006) and his last collection *The Face Of It* (Carcanet, 2007).

ANDREW BREWERTON
Honorary professor of fine art at Shanghai University, Andrew Brewerton worked for a decade in glass crystal manufacturing and design and has been professor of glass at Wolverhampton University and principal of Dartington College of Arts; he has also taught in Italy, Australia and South Africa. He is now principal of Plymouth College of Art. His poetry publications include *Raag Leaves for Paresh Chakraborty* (Exeter: Shearsman Books, 2008). 'The Stoveplate' first appeared in a privately published collection for R.F. Langley's 60th birthday; it concerns an incident in Cratfield church during a shared Suffolk holiday.

RODNEY PYBUS
Rodney Pybus, born in Newcastle in 1938, began publishing his poetry in British magazines in the late 1960s. His first collection was the award-winning *In Memoriam Milena* (London: Chatto & Windus, 1973). He was closely associated from 1964 with the literary quarterly *Stand*, being for many years its co-editor. In the 1960s and 1970s he worked in the north-east of England as a newspaper journalist and a producer-writer in television; he has since lectured at a university in Sydney, been Northern Arts literature officer in the Lake District and taught creative writing, A-level English literature and media studies in schools, universities, colleges and a hospital. He has lived in Sudbury, Suffolk since 1983. His most recent collection, *Darkness Inside Out* (Manchester: Carcanet/Inside Out, 2012), was his first for 18 years.

CHARLOTTE GEATER
Ipswich-born Charlotte Geater is the only poet in this anthology without a full-length individual collection to her name, but it cannot be long before that is rectified. She wrote the poems that provided the titles for the *Foyles Young Poets of the Year* anthologies in both 2005 and 2006; more recently, her work has featured in *The Mays 2010: The Best New Writing, Art and Photography from Oxford and Cambridge*, and in *The Salt Book of Younger Poets*, edited by Roddy Lumsden and Eloise Stonborough.

ZOË SKOULDING
Editor of the international quarterly *Poetry Wales*, Zoë Skoulding teaches English at Bangor University. Her work as a poet encompasses sound-based vocal performance, collaboration and translation; her most recent collection is *Remains of a Future City* (Bridgend: Seren, 2008). She is a member of the collective *Parking Non-Stop*, combining experimental soundscape with poetry and song. Though born in Bradford, she grew up in Flixton, near Bungay, and returns to Suffolk frequently to visit her mother.

DERYN REES-JONES
Director of graduate studies in English at Liverpool University, Deryn Rees-Jones is the author of books on Carol Ann Duffy (Tavistock: Northcote House

Publishers, 1999) and modern women poets, and the editor of *Modern Women Poets* (Tarset: Bloodaxe Books, 2006). Her most recent collection, *Burying the Wren* (Bridgend: Seren Books, 2012) was shortlisted for the T.S. Eliot Prize.

AIDAN SEMMENS
The editor of this anthology is a freelance journalist and photographer who has lived in Suffolk since 1995. He co-edited the magazine *Perfect Bound* 1977-78 and his first pamphlet of poetry was printed at that time in the National Poetry Society basement. His first full-length collection, *A Stone Dog* (Exeter: Shearsman Books, 2011), included the poem *On the Pleasure Beach*, written in 2001, to which one of the poems included here is a sequel; his second book is a sequence of "distressed" sonnets, *The Book of Isaac* (Anderson, SC: Parlor Press / Free Verse Editions 2012).

MICHAEL LASKEY
Michael Laskey founded the international Aldeburgh Poetry Festival in 1989 and directed it through its first decade; he also set up the poetry magazine *Smiths Knoll* with Roy Blackman in 1991 and since Blackman's death in 2002 has been editing it with Joanna Cutts. He has taught at the University of East Anglia, tutors regularly for the Arvon Foundation and works in schools and on writing projects in the wider community. He has lived in Suffolk since 1978. His most recent poetry collection is *The Man Alone* (Sheffield: Smith/Doorstop, 2008).

HERBERT LOMAS
Herbert Lomas (1924-2011) was a regular contributor, as poet and critic, to several publications, notably *Ambit* and *The London Magazine*. His poetry, at various times bawdy, jocular or tender, based on reminiscence or observation, often has a very strong sense of place, be it the Yorkshire Pennines, where he was born and grew up, India, where he served in the Army, London, where he taught at Borough Road College, or Aldeburgh, where he spent his retirement; it was praised by such luminaries as W.H. Auden, Robert Graves, Ted Hughes and Anthony Thwaite. His ten previous collections are gathered together in *A Casual Knack of Living* (Todmorden: Arc Publications 2009). He was named a Knight of the Order of the White Rose of Finland in recognition of his many translations from Finnish.

ANNE BERESFORD
One reviewer of her *Collected Poems* wrote, "The ground beneath Anne Beresford's feet is rural East Anglia"; more specifically, one might describe that ground as coastal east Suffolk, where she has lived and written since 1976—though she has herself said that she 'began publishing her poetry as a Londoner'. Her *Collected Poems 1967-2006* (London: Katabasis, 2006) draws together all she wished to keep from 13 previous collections. She has also translated poetry

from Romanian, including *Alexandros, Selected Poems* by Vera Lungu (Mayfield, E. Sussex: Agenda Editions 1974).

WILL STONE
Will Stone has likened himself to Michael Hamburger as "a European maverick", though much of his poetry, like Hamburger's, is stamped very strongly with the mark of coastal Suffolk, where he was born and now again lives. His first collection, *Glaciation* (Cambridge: Salt Publishing, 2007), won the international Glen Dimplex Award for poetry in 2008. His second, *Drawing in Ash*, was published by Salt in 2011. He has also published translations of the Austrian expressionist Georg Trakl, and Belgian symbolists Emile Verhaeren and Georges Rodenbach.

RICHARD CADDEL
A quietly significant figure in poetry in the north-east of England, Richard Caddel (1949-2003) was influential not only through his own writing and editing. Pig Press, which he ran with his wife Ann, published many of the late 20th century's most interesting modernist or avant-garde writers. For many years he ran poetry readings, first at the Morden Tower in Newcastle, and then in Durham, where he was director of the Basil Bunting Poetry Centre. His selected poems, *Magpie Words*, appeared in 2002 from West House Books, Sheffield, also the publisher of his last collection, *Writing in the Dark* (2003), which includes the poem 'Shiner', reprinted here. His parents lived for some years at Blythburgh, and Ann writes of the poem: "I know he was thinking of Blythburgh church and remembering how Tom [their son, who died in 1995] used to go out on walks by himself round the village at night."

MICHAEL HAMBURGER
Born in Berlin, Michael Hamburger (1924-2007) moved to London with his family in 1933 in the first wave of emigrations from Nazi Germany. He would later become as well known for his translations of such writers as Friedrich Hölderlin, Rainer Maria Rilke, Bertolt Brecht and Hans Magnus Enzensberger—and the letters and journals of Beethoven—as for his own original poetry, though his *Collected Poems 1941-1994* (London: Anvil Press Poetry, 1995) brought together work from a large number of previous books. It covers a remarkably wide range of subjects and styles, but is imbued throughout with his love of nature and a humane, critical eye. Recurrent themes in his later poems are aging and the landscapes and life of Suffolk, where he lived from 1976 with his wife, Anne Beresford. Among his prose works was *The Truth of Poetry* (London: Weidenfeld & Nicholson, 1969). His last collection of poetry was *Circling the Square* (Anvil, 2007).

Acknowledgements

All poems remain copyright of their authors and/or their estates and are used with permission.

'At Sizewell' is taken from *Fall of the Rebel Angels: Poems 1996-2006* by Andy Brown (Cambridge: Salt Publishing, 2006); 'Pine trees at Five Ways' is taken from *Goose Music* by Andy Brown and John Burnside (Salt, 2008).

'Scallop' and 'Station' are from *The Messages* by Angela Leighton (Nottingham: Shoestring Press, 2012).

'The Butley Ferry' appeared in *Fetch* by Tamar Yoseloff (Cambridge: Salt Publishing 2007).

'Down to the Dwelling House' is taken from *At The Yeoman's House* by Ronald Blythe (London: Enitharmon Press, 2011).

'Sayer', 'Iceni' and 'Shrill Water' are taken from *Flatlands* by Victor Tapner (London: Salt Publishing, 2010).

'Little Egypt' and 'Lepers at Dunwich' appear in *The Lady & the Hare, New & Selected Poems* by Pauline Stainer (Tarset: Bloodaxe Books 2003).

'Rivers' appears in *Collected Longer Poems* by John Matthias (Bristol: Shearsman Books, 2012) and 'Kedging' in *Collected Shorter Poems Vol. 2* by John Matthias (Shearsman 2011).

'At Thorpeness' and 'The Question' come from *The Land Between* by Wendy Mulford (Hastings: Reality Street Editions, 2009).

'Warrener' appears in *Stretch of Closures* by Claire Crowther (Exeter: Shearsman Books, 2007).

'The Ecstasy Inventories' is taken from *Collected Poems* by R.F. Langley (Manchester: Carcanet Press, 2000).

'Silly Season' and 'Spitting Distance' are taken from *Flying Blues* by Rodney Pybus (Manchester: Carcanet Press, 1994). 'Speaking of Angels' by Rodney Pybus appeared in *Light Unlocked: Christmas Card Poems*, edited by Kevin Crossley-Holland & Lawrence Sail (London: Enitharmon Press, 2005)

'Midnight Beach at Sizewell B' is taken from *Signs Round a Dead Body* by Deryn Rees-Jones (Bridgend: Seren Books 1998).

'The Corpse' is taken from *Permission to Breathe* by Michael Laskey (Huddersfield: Smith/Doorstop Books 2004); 'Close' is taken from *The Man Alone: New and Selected Poems* by Michael Laskey (Sheffield: Smith/Doorstop Books, 2008).

'The Wild Swans at Aldeburgh', 'Sea Lady' and 'Night Fishing' are taken from *A Casual Knack of Living: Collected Poems* by Herbert Lomas (Todmorden: Arc Publications, 2009).

'The Chariot' and 'Suffolk Future' are taken from *Collected Poems 1967-2006* by Anne Beresford (London: Katabasis, 2006).

'Reeds in November' and 'Greyfriars' are taken from *Glaciation* by Will Stone (Cambridge: Salt Publishing, 2007).

'Shiner' is taken from *Writing In The Dark* by Richard Caddel (Sheffield: West House Books, 2003) and is copyright © The Estate of Richard Caddel.

'In the Country' is taken from *Collected Poems 1941-1994* by Michael Hamburger (London: Anvil Press Poetry, 1995); 'Winter Evenings, East Suffolk' is taken from *Circling the Square: Poems 2004-2006* by Michael Hamburger (Anvil, 2007).